UNDERGROUND
HALIFAX

Edited by Paul A. Erickson

NIMBUS
PUBLISHING

Nimbus Publishing Limited
PO Box 9166
Halifax, NS   B3K 5M8
(902) 455-4286

Printed and bound in Canada

Design: Min Landry

Note: *Sidebars written by: Robert Plowman (RP), Sophie Martin (SM), Paul Erickson (PE), Dawn Erickson (DE), Laird Niven (LN), Greg Cochkanoff (GC), Gordon Fader (GF)*

Library and Archives Canada Cataloguing in Publication

Underground Halifax : stories of archaeology in the city
/ edited by Paul Erickson.
Includes bibliographical references.
ISBN 1-55109-527-0

1. Halifax (N.S.)—Antiquities. 2. Excavations (Archaeology)
—Nova Scotia—Halifax. I. Erickson, Paul A.
FC2346.39.U52 2005   971.6'225   C2005-902424-0

We acknowledge the financial support of the Government of Canada through the Book Publishing Industry Development Program (BPIDP) and the Canada Council, and of the Province of Nova Scotia through the Department of Tourism, Culture and Heritage for our publishing activities.

Dedicated to the exuberant memory of
John Andrew Harvey (1981–2005)

Contents

Foreword

A precious record of Halifax's history remains hidden. When discovered piece by piece, it helps us to understand who we are and where we came from. These are our archaeological treasures. Archaeologists are both treasure seekers and the guardians of these collective memories, where the hidden evidence of our past resides.

Halifax is one of Canada's oldest settlements, founded in 1749, and the city's rich archaeological record is an integral part of our nation's heritage—reflecting the work of its settlers and the lifestyle of its citizens.

Halifax is to English Canada what Quebec City is to French Canada. It was here that British culture first established a presence in our country, save for outport settlements in Newfoundland and military outposts in Annapolis Royal.

In 1749, nearly two thousand colonists led by Governor Edward Cornwallis hacked a settlement out of virgin growth on the shores of Halifax Harbour to serve as a British military outpost to counter Louisbourg. Halifax later recorded the immigration of the Planters in the 1760s, the Loyalists after 1784, the Irish, Scots, and English from the British Isles, and Blacks from southern climates. It experienced privateering during the Napoleonic Wars, hosted innumerable ships during the Age of Sail, and harboured Confederate sympathizers during the American Civil War. It has a rich history.

Much of the evidence of those more than 250 years, as well as earlier years of First Nations habitation, has been lost and is now covered by the sediment of progress. However, archaeologists can mine these fertile veins to produce the valuable ore of our history—a history that is unique in Canada.

Underground Halifax brings together a selection of some of the most interesting and varied archaeological undertakings in Halifax. This book shares these exciting discoveries of our history with a broad public, reminding us that these treasures belong not only to the people of Halifax, but to all Canadians.

Paul Erickson is the first scholar to assemble a collection of the archaeological adventures in Halifax. It is a task long overdue and one which his special knowledge of this field and his intimate familiarity with Halifax's history have especially fitted him to carry out. He has selected a rich blend of archaeological events in the city's history and assembled them with the industry and accuracy that is essential for serious study. Anyone with a curiosity about our past, as well as scholars, antiquarians, historians, and archaeologists, will find this an inspiring treasury of the discovery of Halifax's hidden secrets.

Alan V. Parish
President, Heritage Trust of Nova Scotia

Introduction

Paul A. Erickson, Saint Mary's University

Archaeology in Halifax? Yes, and lots of it; or at least more than you might think. There have been more than two hundred archaeology projects in the Halifax Regional Municipality. That volume of work puts Halifax on the edge of the rapidly expanding global enterprise of conducting archaeology in urban centres.

Archaeology in Cities

The popular image of archaeologists is that they work in exotic locations to unearth remains of exotic peoples. Contrary to this stereotype, many archaeologists work close to home to uncover remains left virtually in their own back yards, in the cities of Canada, the United States, and Europe. Although archaeologists have always been interested in cities, this interest was once confined to the cities of ancient civilizations, such as those of the Egyptians, Greeks, Romans, and Chinese. Now, the emerging interest in modern cities has generated a new field: urban archaeology. Urban archaeologists face many challenges, because digging in modern cities can be complicated. Still, there are extraordinary rewards involved in this kind of work, because underneath modern cities there is often a wealth of invaluable artifacts (objects that were intentionally manufactured, like crockery and glassware) and features (things that were manufactured but cannot be easily excavated, like foundations and drainage systems) awaiting discovery. Furthermore, because modern cities belong to literate cultures, urban archaeologists have recourse to written documents to aid them in their search and interpretation. That is why urban archaeology is part of what is called historical archaeology, in contrast with the pre-historical—or pre-(European) contact—archaeology of most First Nations cultures.

Urban archaeology has grown along with a curiosity about how cities have evolved. The archaeology *of* cities, which refers mainly to this growing interest in urbanization, is usually accompanied by the realization that construction in cities is likely to damage archaeological remains. The attempt to mitigate, or minimize, this damage has made urban archaeology part of the governmental strategy for cultural resources management. Archaeology *in* cities refers mainly to archaeology conducted for this purpose. Urban archaeology in Halifax has involved archaeology both *of* and *in* the city, with archaeologists trying to keep one step ahead of development.

Archaeology in Halifax

Predating the founding of Halifax, the first inhabitants of the area were First Nations people, including the Mi'kmaq. In this book, David Christianson details the archaeological evidence of their presence, which dates back eleven thousand years. His story involves rock carvings in Bedford, a mysterious artifact from Dartmouth, and a burial mound in White's Lake.

First to conduct systematic archaeology in Halifax was the Canadian Parks Service (or Parks Canada), which maintains archaeological jurisdiction over federal land in the city. Beginning in earnest in the 1970s, Parks Canada undertook the archaeological investigation of military installations, including those on Citadel Hill and Georges Island. Earl Luffman examines the archaeological record of Fort George and Fort Charlotte at these respective locations. His historical dramatization of the day in a Quartermaster Sergeant's life at each site depicts the challenges of supplying water and discharging sewage at the forts in their early days.

Outside of federal jurisdiction, the advent of archaeology in Halifax dates to 1984, when passersby noticed that workmen were unearthing old artifacts during the construction of the Central Trust (now HSBC) office tower at the corner of Hollis and George streets. A hasty effort by city officials and civic-minded Haligonians led to a temporary reprieve from the backhoes, providing a brief window of opportunity for a team of Saint Mary's University volunteers to salvage what they could. April D. MacIntyre and Stephen A. Davis tell this exciting story, contrasting it with archaeological investigations at the construction site of a nearby Halifax parkade seventeen years later.

While salvaging artifacts can be worthwhile (more than twenty-five thousand artifacts were salvaged from the Central Trust site), salvaging by itself is far from ideal. When artifacts are wrenched out of context, much of their value for illuminating the social history of a site is lost. Archaeologists are able to interpret artifacts much better if the artifacts are found *in situ* (in their original location). Locating artifacts and features in situ usually requires that archaeological investigations take place before construction begins. And for that to happen, everyone involved in a construction project needs to know ahead of time where artifacts and features might be found. In 1985, in the wake of the Central Trust affair, the city of Halifax, realizing the importance of proactive research, hired Nicola Hubbard to identify areas of the city with high archaeological potential. Increasingly, this has been the approach taken by scores of modern cities interested in preserving archaeological heritage in a way that minimizes potential disruptions to construction schedules.

Although Hubbard's recommendations were not implemented in Halifax, in 1986, another team of volunteers from Saint Mary's and I undertook to show the value of proactive research by pin-pointing the location of an eighteenth-century North End cottage, which they then verified through archaeological excavation. Dawn T. Erickson tells the story of finding this cottage, which belonged to the grandmother of pioneer Haligonian Samuel Sellon.

The Central Trust affair helped to raise awareness of the wealth of archaeological treasures that remain buried throughout Halifax, especially in historically significant locations. In 1987, aiming to promote the importance of archaeology in the province, a group of concerned citizens formed the Nova Scotia Archaeology Society, comprising both professional archaeologists and a variety of "amateurs," better known as avocational archaeologists. In 1989, the society staged an international conference called Doing Urban Archaeology. Held in Halifax, the conference brought together representatives of four cities operating different kinds of urban archaeology programs. In Alexandria, Virginia, archaeology is conducted by a community-based organization that draws on a cross-section of the citizenry and operates a museum with opportunities for visitors to engage in archaeology firsthand. In New York City, where archaeologists are paid municipal employees, the strategy is to entice land developers to support archaeology in the understanding that it will ultimately make development simpler and less expensive. In Quebec City, archaeologists enjoy support that comes from widespread recognition that their work, which helped restore Old Quebec, enhances the appeal of the city to tourists. And in Toronto, an archaeology program (now defunct) involved hundreds of public school teachers and students who participated in "digs" and post-excavation laboratory analysis. After listening to these experts, a panel of local stakeholders discussed which elements of the four programs might be implemented in Halifax. The stakeholders represented developers, city employees, archivists, historians, university-based archaeologists, private-sector contract archaeologists, avocational archaeologists, and the Nova Scotia Museum, the institution responsible for regulating archaeology in the province. Following the conference, the Archaeology Society formulated a plan for a preliminary urban archaeology program, which they proposed to Halifax City Council. Citing lack of money, council turned the proposal down.

Archaeology and Legislation

It was a few years earlier, in 1980, that Nova Scotia first passed legislation governing the conduct of archaeology in the province. Amended in 1989, the *Special Places Protection Act* provides for the investigation, preservation, and regulation of paleontological, ecological, and archaeological sites. If a site is extraordinarily important, the province can designate it a "special place" and grant it extraordinary protection. In reality, only a few sites in Nova Scotia have been declared special places. Indeed, in 2004, only one archaeological site in Halifax had received this protection: Fletcher's Lock, part of the Shubenacadie Canal. Nevertheless, important archaeological provisions of the act apply to all land in the province, including cities, whether designated "special" or not.

In Halifax, and throughout the province, it is illegal for just anyone to dig for archaeological artifacts or features, or even to collect artifacts above ground or from excavations already underway. According to the *Special Places Protection Act*, these artifacts and features belong not to individuals but to the people of Nova Scotia, who have the right to learn what they reveal about their past. What artifacts and features reveal is greatly diminished if they are disturbed or removed from their original location without prior and proper archaeological investigation. For these reasons, anyone wishing to conduct archaeology in Halifax must obtain permission from the Nova Scotia Museum.

Acting on behalf of all Nova Scotians, the museum regulates archaeology through a system of permits. Whether on public or private land, anyone undertaking archaeology or any other activity—including land development—with the known potential to disturb archaeological remains must first obtain a permit. Furthermore, if any activity reveals previously unknown archaeological remains, that activity must stop, at least temporarily, and an archaeological assessment must be conducted. Fines for infractions of these regulations can range from ten thousand dollars for individuals to one hundred thousand dollars for corporations. There are permits for surface investigation without excavation, for excavation motivated by academic research, and for excavation in order to assess the archaeological impact of proposed development. All permits carry with them stipulations for the qualifications of personnel, record keeping and reporting, and the care of recovered artifacts, which are to be turned over to the Nova Scotia Museum for custody.

The *Special Places Protection Act* also governs land underwater, where there can be sites of former human habitation, particularly habitation by First Nations peoples, as well as accumulated debris and remains of maritime activity, notably shipwrecks. In certain circumstances, another provincial act, the *Treasure Trove Act*, allows individuals and corporations to dive on wrecks to recover and retain precious stones and metals, as long as they pay a provincial royalty. Yet another provincial act, the *Cemeteries Protection Act*, provides for the protection, disposition, and appropriate accessibility of abandoned cemeteries. In addition to these acts, some environmental protection legislation mandates archaeological investigation, which is then conducted under the provincial permit system. In Halifax, there are no special municipal archaeology bylaws or official policies governing archaeology. Therefore, archaeology in the city derives from provincial legislation, often implemented after lobbying by interested parties and dependent on bureaucratic and political good will.

Archaeology Tools

Urban archaeologists employ a wide range of investigative techniques and tools, from high-tech computers to low-tech shovels, trowels, and toothbrushes. Before beginning work, they want to know as much as possible about what they might find. Once an archaeological feature or artifact is uncovered, they want to identify it and figure out its place in the past. For guidance in these tasks, archaeologists turn to archivists. In 1992, Liam D. Murphy compiled an archival guide book for Halifax archaeologists, showing how to access maps, plans, photographs, deeds, wills, and other documentary material housed at the Nova Scotia Registry of Deeds and Nova Scotia Archives and Records Management. Murphy drew upon this material to reconstruct the exciting history behind an unassuming, nearly vacant block of prime downtown real estate, then ripe for redevelopment. A decade later, with sophisticated computers, Danny Dyke used Geographical Information System (GIS) software to digitally superimpose modern maps onto historical maps of downtown Halifax. He identified precise locations of many former residential and military structures—before archaeologists ever broke ground. In this book, both Murphy and Dyke describe and update their work and explain how it helps to bring history to life.

Archaeology and Development

A goal of urban archaeology is to provide information to land developers to help minimize damage to archeological remains. Of course, developments vary greatly and range from small- to extraordinarily large-scale. From 1996 to 1998, Paul Williams co-led a team of archaeological investigators in protecting the human remains buried in three crypts beneath the Little Dutch Church on Brunswick Street. Before the church underwent restoration, Williams and his team temporarily removed the remains for safekeeping. In the process, they identified the decedents and discovered more burials in a mysterious mass grave, probably dating back to 1750. Beginning in 2001, Bruce Stewart led an archaeological investigation of an entire city block in Halifax's North End. The block, once a bustling community, was then vacant and slated to become the site of a wastewater treatment plant. In 2004, Fred Schwarz and Lynne Schwarz conducted an archaeological survey of Point Pleasant Park in order to identify archaeological features that needed protection during cleanup of the devastation caused by Hurricane Juan. In these three cases, archaeologists allowed restoration, development, and cleanup to proceed. In another case, recounted by Michele Raymond, researchers documented the existence of military and civilian installations on Deadmans Island in Halifax's Northwest Arm. This documentation—and the international media attention it garnered—contributed to the withdrawal of a proposed residential development on the land in question, creating an opportunity for investigative archaeology to be carried out in the future.

Helping History

Archaeology is sometimes called the handmaiden of history. This label recognizes the ability of archaeology to enhance, or sometimes correct, the historical record by revealing physical evidence that has otherwise gone unrecorded. Once revealed, this evidence can aid historical interpretation. For more than two decades, Stephen Davis and other archaeologists, including April McIntyre, have been investigating the old Shubenacadie Canal, an ambitious and visionary engineering experiment to link Halifax Harbour with the Minas Basin. In collaboration with historians and canal experts they have explored a settlement of Irish laborers and unmasked the workings of canal locks and the Portobello inclined plane. Meanwhile, in 1992, Katie Cottreau-Robins archaeologically unearthed traces of the razed Seaview United Baptist Church in Africville, a former black community on the shores of Bedford Basin. Cottreau-Robins's work yielded the information necessary to construct a church replica, which the provincial government agreed to support. As a result of these various investigations, the past can be reconstructed for present enjoyment, education, and commemoration.

Grassroots Archaeology

The demographic appeal of archaeology is broad, with people everywhere, of all ages, and from all walks of life anxious to participate. Across North America, archaeology is taught in all kinds of schools, sometimes even to students as young as nine or ten years old. In 1993, the Nova Scotia Archaeology Society published *Discovering Archaeology: An Activity Book for Young Nova Scotians*, distributing thousands of copies to enthusiastic teachers and students. And archaeology has not simply made its way onto the public-school reading list. Many cities, including Toronto, have capitalized on a sizeable pool of available talent and labour to operate hands-on archaeology programs through schools. In 1994, the Nova Scotia Archaeology Society, the Rockingham Historical Society, and Halifax West High School teamed up to excavate the site of the Rockingham Inn, a former military barracks in Rockingham that in the 1800s became a gathering place for Halifax's social elite. Teacher David Williamson involved other experts in setting up and operating an archaeology laboratory at the school. Elsewhere in Halifax, archaeologist Laird Niven helped teachers and students at J. L. Illsley High School unearth buried buildings at Coote Cove, a former fishing village near Crystal Crescent Beach. The two field schools were a great success, attracting corporate sponsorship, a national curriculum award, and extensive media coverage. Halifax teachers and students have also contributed to the archaeology at the Little Dutch Church, Africville, and several other sites.

Halifax Underwater

With its extensive coastline and rich maritime history, Halifax hosts a bounty of underwater archaeological treasures. However, underwater archaeology presents its own set of challenges, with special procedures, precautions, equipment, and personnel. Scuba diver Greg Cochkanoff has located sherds of broken china emblazoned with steamship company house flags and ornate naval insignia. He has created an extensive steamship china catalogue that chronicles transatlantic navigation and the importance of Halifax as a seaport and naval base. And marine geologist Gordon Fader has conducted an underwater survey of Halifax Harbour, using sophisticated imaging technology transported in a miniature submarine. In addition to shipwrecks, he has located submerged islands and remains of the first Halifax Harbour bridges.

Underground Halifax, then, presents sixteen different stories of archaeology in the city. These stories sample many more that could be told—and might be told in the future, as archaeology in Halifax continues to expand.

First Nations Archaeology in Halifax

David Christianson
Nova Scotia Museum of Natural History

THE STORY OF FIRST NATIONS ARCHAEOLOGY in Halifax Regional Municipality is fascinating and complex. It is a story that begins with the first people to enter Nova Scotia, more than eleven thousand years ago. It highlights the Mi'kmaw people, who were encountered by Europeans, Africans, and others who settled in Halifax after 1749. These later settlers came to occupy lands that had been named, visited, inhabited, and respected since the last Ice Age.

How We Know What We Know

We begin the story with a 1791 watercolour painting by Hibbert Newton Binney (1766–1842), a collector of impost and excise (taxes) for the port of Halifax. The water-colour depicts Mi'kmaw individuals returning home with a cod catch, creating a splint bas-ket, and simply enjoying each other's company. We know from Binney that the depicted location was somewhere along the Dartmouth shoreline, perhaps near Tuft's Cove. His painting captures one moment in a First Nation's land-use pattern that spans thousands of years. It also documents the existence of a Mi'kmaw settlement forty-two years after the beginning of the colonial settlement of Halifax.

An extensive glossary of place names also documents Mi'kmaw familiarity with the land. Harry Piers compiled the glossary by conversing with Jerry Lonecloud. Piers, curator from 1899 to 1941 of what is now the Nova Scotia Museum, was an expert recorder of museum collections, and his work is a major source of information about early archaeology in Nova Scotia. Lonecloud, born Germain Laski, was a Mi'kmaw legend keeper, performer, guide, and herbalist. He collected artifacts and natural his-tory specimens for the museum and shared his knowledge of Mi'kmaw culture with Piers, and the two sustained a twenty-year professional relationship and friendship.

From Lonecloud, Piers learned that Chebooktook ("long harbour") was the name for Bedford Basin (the variant "Chebucto" has survived in more general use in English today); Gwowaqmicktook ("white pine forest"), the landscape of peninsular Halifax; Dwidden ("the big passage"), the main entrance to Halifax Harbour; and El-pay-sok-ticht ("leaning towards the sea") and El-pay-gwitck ("turned-over, like a pot"), McNabs and Georges Islands, respectively. The name of a place in Fairview was Al-e-sool-a-way-ga-deek ("at the place of the measles"), recalling the tragic death of many Mi'kmaq from disease transmitted by the French, perhaps during the Duke D'Anville expedition of 1746.

Archaeological sites can add substantially to this understanding of past First Nations settlement and land use. Just as paintings and language are repositories of visual and descriptive information, archaeological sites are like archives for the physical remains of past lives. Archaeologists study the tools people made, used, and discarded, as well as the dwellings people lived in and the patterns of distribution of their houses across the land-

Previous Page: This watercolour and pencil and ink image of a Mi'kmaw encampment in Dartmouth, c.1791, was created by Hibbert Newton Binney.

2

scape. Archaeologists find and analyze remains of food in order to help define ecosystems. In these and other ways, they use physical evidence to reveal past human activities.

Archaeological sites are ephemeral and incomplete—people do not neatly prepare all of their possessions for archaeologists to discover in the future. Added to the challenges of finding and interpreting dispersed material remains is the deterioration caused by climate and soil conditions. The soils of Nova Scotia are naturally acidic, contributing to the decomposition of most objects made from organic materials such as wood or bone, and coastal erosion has been a problem for thousands of years. Many First Nations archaeological sites formerly located along the shoreline have been washed away because of erosion. Some of these eroded sites, like one located just off Digby Neck, are known to us because fishing draggers have recovered artifacts from the ocean bottom. Other sites, in places like Mahone Bay and Merigomish Island, were reported in the nineteenth century, but have by now been substantially eroded by storm action and rising sea levels. Nevertheless, in spite of these problems, archaeological evidence has survived. Surviving archaeological sites and artifacts are true time capsules, allowing us to glimpse aspects of life in Nova Scotia beginning shortly after the retreat of the last glacial ice sheets.

View of Dartmouth, *1819, a watercolour by G. Childs.*

The Archaeological Evidence

Archaeologists divide First Nations history into broad periods that reflect major environmental conditions and corresponding human economic and social adaptations. They use the forms of artifacts and other physical evidence to define these periods. For eastern North America, they define four periods: adapted for the Maritime Provinces, they are the Palaeo Period (11,000 to 9,000 years ago); Archaic Period (9,000 to 2,500 years ago); Maritime Woodland, or Ceramic, Period (2,500 to 500 years ago); and Post-(European) Contact Period (500 years ago to the present). The Post-Contact Period comprises the time of sustained contact between the Mi'kmaq and newcomers from overseas. There is evidence of First Nations activities in what is now urban Halifax from each of these four periods.

Palaeo Period

The Palaeo Period in Halifax Regional Municipality is represented by a single artifact, discovered by resident Adam Chambers in 1986 at the height of land overlooking Red Bridge Pond in Dartmouth. The artifact, called the Chambers point, is a form of stone

Above: These ground stone artifacts date from what archaeologists call the Palaeo and Archaic periods of First Nations history.

Below: These artifacts from Adam Esson and from the Stora Site date from what archaeologists call the Maritime Woodland Period of First Nations history.

tool that archaeologists call a bifacial preform ("bifacial" means that the stone is worked on both sides nearly symmetrically, and preform denotes that the tool was made only incompletely). The biface is an isolated find, an artifact found without other artifacts or other evidence of human activity. The Palaeo Period marks the beginning of human settlement in the Halifax Regional Municipality. Despite disruptions from land development, it is possible that other Palaeo Period sites remain in the area, awaiting discovery. Countless Haligonians may have walked over them, just like First Nations residents did eleven thousand years ago.

Archaic Period

The Archaic Period coincided with dramatic changes in climate, vegetation, and animal communities. Coastal water levels began to rise, and the configuration of Halifax Harbour, Bedford Basin, and the adjacent rivers and lake systems approached their present forms. We know from evidence uncovered elsewhere in Nova Scotia and northeastern North America that this was a period of increasing cultural complexity. There are Archaic archaeological sites reported along the river and lake systems surrounding urban Halifax, but there are only a few Archaic artifacts from urban areas themselves. Most of these artifacts were found in the early decades of the twentieth century and documented by researchers such as Harry Piers.

The Archaic period introduced a new method for making tools, called "ground stone technology." Artifacts such as axes, adzes, and gouges were produced by intensive grinding of suitable stones. The illustration shows a 2,300-year-old axe or maul attributed to the Susquehanna Tradition, a cultural adaptation appearing in the Susquehanna River Valley in the northeastern United States. An influx of Susquehanna cultural traits, and probably a migration of Susquehanna people, occurred in the northeast at this time, although it is unclear whether the migration reached Nova Scotia. The artifacts from this tradition found in Nova Scotia may have been traded into the area.

Maritime Woodland Period

The Maritime Woodland, or Ceramic, Period begins with the introduction of pottery and pottery making by the First Nations people in the Maritime Provinces. One of the most intriguing artifacts in the collection of the Nova Scotia Museum is from the early part of this period. It was found in 1837 near what is now Admiralty Place, and a local newspaper reported the discovery:

> A spear head about six inches long, made of flint—and two pieces of hollow tube of the same material, finely polished, were found at Dartmouth a day or two since, by persons digging a cellar. They are evidently of Indian manufacture—and are interesting curiosities—having very probably been fashioned at the hands of Aborigines, either before the discovery of this country by the Whites, or during early attempts at settlement. They are now in the possession of Mr. Adam Esson, who will, we dare say, finally deposit them in the Museum of the Mechanics' Institute. (Martin, 195)

The fate of the spearhead is unknown, but the artifact described as "two pieces of hollow tube" became part of the Mechanics' Institute's collection of models and specimens. In 1868, the collection was transferred to the Provincial Museum, and later Harry Piers described the artifact and speculated on how it might have been made. Archaeologists now know that the artifact is a blocked-end tubular pipe. It is made from Ohio pipestone and associated with the archaeological Middlesex complex, from between 2,600 and 2,100 years ago. Archaeologists define a complex as a group of distinctive artifacts and traits that occur in archaological sites within a restricted area over a specified period of time, and they describe this complex as an "interaction sphere," wherein peoples throughout eastern North America traded goods regularly and perhaps also shared religious beliefs and spiritual values. The Middlesex complex in turn was strongly influenced by the archaeological Adena

FIRST KNOWN SETTLEMENT IN NOVA SCOTIA

The somewhat unassuming location of Debert near Truro, Nova Scotia, holds a fascinating archeological treasure: it is the only site in the Maritime provinces to show evidence of a major living area of the Palaeo-Indians, who were the first humans in this region. Palaeo-Indians, who lived in Nova Scotia as far back as eleven thousand years ago, were nomadic hunters of big game and would have followed the retreat of the glaciers northward, bringing them from the rest of North America into what is now eastern Canada. Debert contains many artifacts that point to a thriving Paleo-Indian culture. Distinct living areas, complete with hearths and charcoal, have been unearthed, alongside assortments of stone lance points, awls, stone spoke shaves and abraders (tools used to form spears), and prepared stone scrapers for scraping and cleaning animals hides. Due to the climate and location of the site, it is hypothesized that these early people were hunters of caribou and over-wintering clusters of harp seal. However, due to rising coastlines, all clear evidence of activity on the shore has long since been erased. It is believed that about ten and a half thousand years ago, encroaching glaciers associated with the Younger Dryas Event climatic cooling created conditions that made human survival imposible, and Nova Scotia's settled Palaeo-Indian Period population relocated to warmer climates. –SM

Cultural tradition, centered in the Ohio River Valley of the United States. Middlesex artifacts are often found associated with places of human burial, as was almost certainly the case at what is now called the Esson site.

A second remarkable archaeological discovery associated with the Middlesex tradition was also accidental. The Skora site in White's Lake was discovered in 1986 by two joggers, one of whom happened to be trained in archaeology. Distinctive stone artifacts were noted on the ground surface where a small knoll had been cut off by bulldozers to fill in a roadbed adjacent to new subdivided building lots. The Nova Scotia Museum and Saint Mary's University were notified, and, after visiting the site, archaeologists immediately recognized that it belonged to the Middlesex tradition. Because the site was almost certainly a place of human burial, the Mi'kmaq Grand Council and the Mi'kmaq Association of Cultural Studies were asked to help decide how the site should be treated. The decision was made to recover the disturbed human remains for reburial, and then to ascertain the boundaries of the site in order to facilitate its protection. The human remains were reburied by Mi'kmaq Grand Council representatives, and the remaining portion of the Skora Site, now green space, was protected. A bronze plaque marks the site and explains its significance.

These mylar tracings of the Bedford Barrens petroglyphs were created by Ruth Holmes Whitehead.

McNabs Island is the location of a number of archaeological sites relating to First Nations settlement. One site of special interest documents Mi'kmaw settlement and the use of Halifax Harbour resources in the centuries leading up to 1749. The site in question is a Maritime Woodland midden, or refuse dump, consisting of food bones, mollusc shells, discarded tools, and a variety of other artifacts. Middens are especially revealing archaeological sites, because they contain the kind of information required to determine how people in the past interacted with their environment. By studying middens, archaeologists can learn which foods were eaten, how they were prepared, and what time of the year natural resources were used. Archaeologists have conducted a preliminary study of the midden site on McNabs Island, and it is possible that other Mi'kmaw sites are present nearby.

Petroglyphs, or "rock art," are images carved into stone. The best known Mi'kmaw petroglyphs are probably the hundreds of images found at the Kejimkujik National Historic Site, but there are also several petroglyphs in urban areas. The most significant of these lie within the Bedford Barrens, adjacent to a modern housing development.

The Bedford Barrens petroglyphs came to the attention of the Nova Scotia Museum in 1983. In 1990, archaeologist Brian Molyneaux studied the petroglyphs and conducted an archaeological survey of adjacent areas. The petroglyphs are almost certainly Mi'kmaw. There are two principal glyphs: an eight-pointed star and an anthropomorphic, or human-like, figure connected to a smaller glyph interpreted as a vulva. Molyneaux was unable to date the glyphs precisely, but initials carved over one of them appear to predate 1926. The underlying glyphs had probably already eroded to the point of not being clearly visible when the initials were carved. Molyneaux believes that the petroglyphs date to at least before World War One, and perhaps much earlier. Some aspects of the incisions suggest a stone tool may have been used, but the nature of the parent rock makes it difficult to determine for certain whether the tool was stone or metal. If the tool was stone, the petroglyphs could predate the Post-Contact Period.

Spurious Finds

Some early First Nations artifacts have turned out to be spurious. They were not hoaxes, but simply originated somewhere else and were brought to Nova Scotia in recent times—like two strikingly similar artifacts reported to the Nova Scotia Museum eighty-seven years apart. In 2001, an artifact was brought to the museum with very little information other than the donor's belief that its origin was local. The artifact shows that it superficially resembles the ground stone tools made during the Archaic and Maritime Woodland periods; experts at the museum, however, determined that the artifact is really a mid-nineteenth-century "war club" from a First Nations Plains culture in western Canada or the United States. While studying the artifact, the experts learned that in 1914 an extraordinarily similar object had been found on Windmill Road in Dartmouth. At that time, Harry Piers speculated that a traveler had brought the artifact to Dartmouth and either abandoned or lost it. In this case, studying the 2001 object led to the conclusion that Piers's speculation was correct.

These archaeological finds are only a small sample of all the First Nations activities that took place in the Halifax Regional Municipality before it was settled by Europeans. Although urban development has impacted on the First Nations archaeological record, more sites and artifacts undoubtedly remain to be discovered. We all have a role in ensuring that these irreplaceable records of the past are preserved and commemorated. Just as Hibbert Newton Binney captured a moment in the lives of Mi'kmaw people on the Dartmouth shoreline in 1791, First Nations archaeological sites capture otherwise unknown aspects of the lives of ancestors who lived thousands of years ago.

Plumbing the Past
Water and Sewage at
Fort Charlotte and Fort George

Earl Luffman, Parks Canada

I N HALIFAX, THE CHALLENGES of obtaining drinking water and disposing of sewage are not new. These challenges have existed since the founding of the city in 1749. At military installations, the challenges were compounded by the need for confinement and the crowding of large numbers of people into small quarters. In recent decades, archaeologists have begun to understand how these challenges were met at the military installations on Georges Island and Citadel Hill.

The History of Fort Charlotte and Fort George

The oval-shaped hills on which the fortifications at Georges Island (Fort Charlotte) and Citadel Hill (Fort George) are built are the remains of the last glacial age. These glacial hills, known as drumlins, are composed mainly of rock, clay, and sand. This combination of materials, and the hilly shape in which they were deposited, severely tested the patience and skill of military engineers. Historian Joseph Greenough states simply that Citadel Hill was "an inconvenient place to build anything…" (7). But a hill in military planning is like iron attracted to a magnet. This particular magnet attracted at least six Royal Engineer officers, numerous British ministry committees, a military heavyweight in the person of the Duke of Wellington, and, finally, piles of money.

The British government had not intended to spend piles of money. Actually, they had not intended to spend much money at all on fortifications in colonial outposts such as Halifax, especially in peacetime. But sometimes military projects develop a weight of their own, like glaciers, and in August of 1828 construction began on the fourth and most ambitious fort on Citadel Hill (there had been three previous forts), with the intention of completing it within six years at a cost of £116,000. The fourth Fort George was completed twenty-eight years later at a cost of £242,000—and by then it was obsolete. The planning and building of fortifications on Georges Island were not immune to the forces that shaped fortifications on Citadel Hill. Both sites were too small for properly designed and appropriate installations. As a result, both "hills" had to be reduced in height to allow for more flat space on which to construct gun batteries. The initial fortifications at both sites were earthworks supported by hewn logs. Earth and log fortifications have a short life span in Nova Scotia's soggy, wintry climate, and eventually the British authorities realized that if Halifax were to be successfully defended, it needed more permanent fortifications of masonry.

From the outset, a number of military figures, including the Duke of Wellington, had apprehensions about the strategic value of a masonry fort on Citadel Hill. The effective range of smoothbore cannon in the early 1800s was such that gun batteries on the hill could not effectively support the sea batteries (Georges Island and Grand Battery) during a sea-based attack. Indeed, arguments were made that the hill could hardly defend itself and the town from a land-based attack. Up to the 1860s, the various sea

Opposite page: This aerial view of Citadel Hill shows the projecting angles of Fort George, designed to deflect cannon balls.

batteries and land batteries alone would not have been able to defend Halifax successfully. What really guaranteed the successful defense of the settlement was the presence of the Royal Navy.

All this changed by the mid-nineteenth century with the advent of a new breed of gun, called rifle muzzle loaders (RMLs), and a new type of steam-powered warship, the ironclads. At this time, the inner harbour defenses were strengthened, and it may be argued that for a period of about twenty years Halifax was finally in a position to defend itself without the Royal Navy. By 1855, however, York Redoubt began to take a more commanding role in the defense of Halifax, acting as the central and coordinating unit as well as a deterrent to long-range bombardment from enemy vessels. Although Georges Island and Citadel Hill remained fortified up to 1906, when Britain turned the Halifax garrison over to Canada, their time in the sun had passed.

Today, for the most part, the appearance of both forts in their restored states is much as it would have been in the 1880s. But the trace, or footprint, of the two forts is different.

Rifled muzzle loading guns being unloaded at Halifax, c.1873

Citadel Hill was designed for defense against smoothbore guns and their round, solid shot. Its walls have sharp, projecting angles to deflect such shot. The ramparts, or the raised mounds of earth about the masonry walls, protected the guns and the passage of troops and were able to absorb the shot. By the 1860s, however, the masonry walls and ramparts were no match for the larger, more accurate, and faster-moving shells fired from rifled guns. This new gun technology made the design of Citadel Hill obsolete. Because the footprint of the fort was fixed, the only feasible modifications, short of dismantling the fort, were the addition of newer guns and the thickening of the ramparts.

Fort Charlotte, on the other hand, had the unintended "advantages" of neglect and apathy and perhaps a dash of good fortune. In 1794, Fort Charlotte had received a facelift when Prince Edward, Commander-in-Chief at Halifax, leveled the earthwork defenses and built another fort in their place. This decision was a response to the perceived threat that Napoleon Bonaparte presented as he played his war games in Europe. In 1812, Prince Edward's fort was demolished, and a stone Martello Tower— along with the beginning of a stone wall and ditch around all the fortifications—was built in response to territorial ambitions from American "neighbours" to the south. After 1815, when Napoleon and American president James Madison were out of power and office, there was no perceived need to improve and complete the island's fortifications. Moreover, whatever money was available was needed to build Fort George.

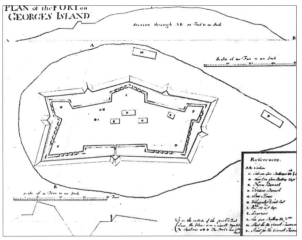

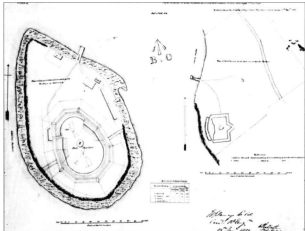

Above left: Plans for Georges Island's first fortress, c.1759
Above right: Fort Charlotte, 1851

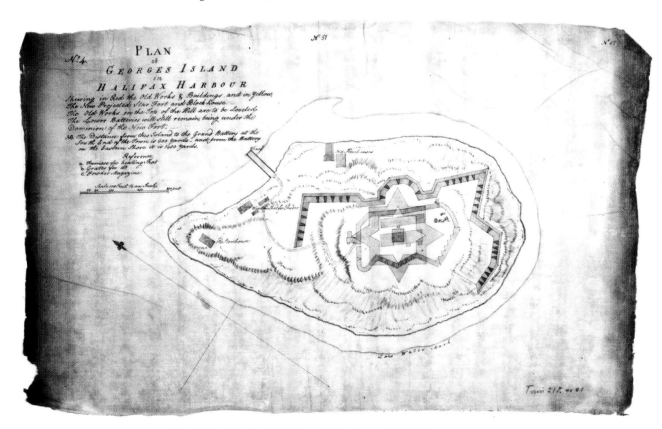

Above: Prince Edward's plan for the new fort on Georges Island, 1794

As a result, by the early 1860s, most of the fortifications on Georges Island were sadly in need of repair. Later, they were rebuilt to both accommodate and withstand the new rifled gun technology. The rebuilt Fort Charlotte had fewer projecting angles but thicker walls and ramparts to absorb rifled shells.

This aerial view of Georges Island shows the walls of Fort Charlotte, designed to absorb rifled shells. They have fewer projecting walls and are thicker than the walls of Fort George on Citadel Hill.

Archaeology at the Forts

Citadel Hill opened as a National Historic Site in 1956, but it was not until 1967 that a comprehensive program of repair and maintenance was proposed. In 1975, a task force recommended that Citadel Hill be restored. Although some archaeological work (mostly salvage work) had been done at Citadel Hill since the early 1960s, more formalized archaeological investigations did not begin until 1976. Archaeological investigations

MILITARY HALIFAX Halifax's rich military history is undeniable, as its initial *raison d'etre* was to defend Nova Scotia, then still a British colony, against the French. Established in 1749, Halifax's vantage point on the largest North American harbour was an ideal location to safeguard against attackers. Though the British had wrested Nova Scotia away from the hands of the French in 1713 due to the Treaty of Utrecht, the region was still greatly unstable, and Britain's enemies would not be long in taking advantage of a weakness. Hence, Halifax's position as a capital was essential to make it a base for military activity, especially as a counterpoint to the ever-present threat of the relatively nearby Fortress of Louisbourg, returned to France in 1748 in the Treaty of Aix-La-Chapelle. –SM continued throughout various phases of the restoration project until the mid-1990s. These investigations had several restoration-related goals, including defining the original military parade composition and elevation, determining the slope and composition of the fort ramparts, and determining the location of gun placements. On Georges Island, formal archaeological investigations began in 1988. There, the major investigations focused on the married quarters, officers' quarters, and features of fortification walls connected to parade composition and drainage.

Water and Sewage

Of all the archaeological investigations at Citadel Hill and Georges Island, those that shed light on how water was obtained and sewage disposed of should be of special interest to Haligonians still struggling to overcome these challenges in the early twenty-first century. Rather than recount these archaeological findings in traditional terms, let us create two fictional historical characters, Bill Alexander and Zachary Aaron, both Brigade Quartermaster Sergeants, and follow them as they conduct their routine inspections of "the facilities." In so doing, we will be telling tales based on real information from archaeological investigations, supplemented by historical research.

Bill's Tale

In the early 1850s, Fort George on Citadel Hill was still a work in progress. Living quarters were scarce, with many soldiers living in off-site barracks. Bill's barracks room, which he shared with fifteen men, was dimly lit with candles, and the early morning fog seemed to exacerbate its dampness. As Bill made his way across the parade to the privy, he stumbled several times. He made a mental note to see that the parade was repaired, but today he hoped to get at the source of complaints about the poor quality of the drinking water coming from the two wells within the fort, and about the noxious odours coming from the privies.

After his usual breakfast of bread and tea, Bill began his inspection of the two wells that supplied all the water for the fort. The wells had serviced the previous forts and were incorporated within the present fort during construction. Bill had heard grumbling about the odours coming from casemate forty-nine, the guardroom adjacent to the main entrance. The guardroom well had been hand-built using random stone construction and was 1.9 metres in diameter and 18.0 metres deep. As Bill removed one of the well covers, he could see matter suspended in the water and several rat holes surrounding the well, and he could easily detect the strong odour. Could the source of the matter and the odour be decomposing rats that had fallen into the well? Bill recorded his observations but knew that the medical authorities would have to be advised before any action was taken. A new water and drainage system for the fort could come none too soon, he thought, and would relieve him of the headaches of these inspections. (It would be several decades before the horrors of the Crimean War and the subsequent work of Florence Nightingale exposed the dangers of inadequate hygiene practices in both military barracks and hospitals.)

The other well, in casemate eighteen near the north passage to a ditch, was deeper and held almost nine hundred thousand litres of water. It was one and a half metres wide at its surface and almost forty-nine metres deep. The well had been built in three stages, with the top stage constructed of dressed granite stones to a depth of about twelve metres. The other two stages were similar in appearance, but with narrower diameters and walls of clay. As Bill entered the well casemate, a brick vaulted room, he

Left: Fort George casemate 18 well. Dressed granite stones were used for the first stage of well construction.

Centre: Fort George soil pit steps, which led to the pit under the west curtain wall privy. The privy contents were removed by bucket through the privy entrance at the base of the steps.

Right: Fort George officers' privy. The opening visible at the centre of the image led to the Citadel's main sewer line. The column on the right was added later to support the privy floor joists.

noticed that the well covers were in place. He removed the covers and recoiled at what he saw: floating on the surface was the body of Sergeant Steward (his real name). Steward had gone missing on December 11, 1850, after an early morning fire had destroyed the Pavilion Barracks, where he had lived with other members of the First Royal Regiment. There was a rumour that Steward had deserted his regiment during the fire-fighting effort. That rumour could now be put to rest—the sergeant had indeed returned to his regiment. Bill surmised the Steward had fallen into the well while directing water removal for fighting the fire. With the water level in the well lowered, it would have been easy for him to have fallen into the well and, in the dark confines of the casemate, gone unnoticed. After the sergeant's bloated body was removed, Bill promised himself that he would be more attentive to future complaints about water quality. (The well was never used for drinking water again.)

The morning inspection was only half completed, and the ranks' and officers' privies still had to be inspected. This was never a pleasant task, especially for the privies of the non-commissioned officers (NCOs), members of other ranks, and women, all of which were located in casemates under the west curtain wall. These soil pits were flushed into a main drain in the west ditch, which flowed towards the harbour side of the fort and eventually connected with the main city drain on Buckingham Street. At this point, the effluent was carried in a pipe or a closed brick drain to the harbour in the area of the Ordnance Yard (near the present Casino Nova Scotia Hotel). The nuisance caused by the monthly flushing of the fort privies moved city fathers to forbid the practice. But the solution, if it could be called that, was no better. A contractor had to descend several steps below the parade surface to gain entrance to the soil pits and shovel the solid waste to a waiting wagon. This "honey wagon" was then driven through the streets of Halifax and emptied into the harbour. The stench from the wagon as it wound its way

through the streets only assured that the sewage problem was neither out of sight nor mind. Still, Bill could remember the old days when he and his barrack mates used a night bucket in the barracks and then, after a quick rinse of the bucket, used it again for washing up. (In 1856, the privies were hand-flushed with water into cesspits in the ditch and then to three cesspits on the western slope of the hill below the perimeter road. In 1862, the whole system was connected to city sewers.)

The morning fog was dissipating, and Bill was badly in need of some fresh air before inspecting the officers' privy. Because there were fewer officers than members of the other ranks, their facilities did not have the same degree of use nor the same level of odour. This welcome difference may also have been due to the high vaulted ceiling in the officers' privy. The officers' privy was also periodically flushed with water. Although no definitive proof exists, it is believed that water was directed from the rain gutters on the ramparts above the privy. The water was then fed into an iron pipe attached to the retaining wall and re-directed into the soil pit under the privy floorboards.

The officers' soil pit had walls of granite, and the floor was sloped toward the east, above which were three privy stalls. At the bottom of the east wall an opening, 1.0 metre by 0.75 metres, directed the effluent to the main Citadel sewer line, which in turn flowed into the municipal line along Buckingham Street to the harbour. Bill's inspection of the officers' privy was finished and, thankfully, had been uneventful. There had been enough excitement for one morning!

Zachary's Tale

Some years later, near the end of the nineteenth century, Zachary Aaron absentmindedly kicked at a small hump of dirt while taking a break with other NCOs near the artillery shed inside the fort. Within the hump of dirt he noticed several nails. These were not the typical wrought-iron nails used for general construction. They were copper nails, and some of them were clenched, indicating that they were probably used in a door to hold the battens. As he smudged the earth with the toe of his boot, more nails appeared.

Zachary enjoyed solving mysteries. After his break, he led a small squad of artillery men in scouring the area. After all, he rationalized, this was necessary maintenance work. His attention was quickly diverted as a shovel clanged on something solid. With more soil removed, he could see the outline of a curved stone wall. Further digging showed that the wall was actually a stone foundation. But for what? Perhaps he might find out after he finished his other inspections and talked to Sheldon, an artillery sergeant who was an avid reader and history buff. But that would have to wait, because Zachary had to investigate why the officers' privy smelled worse than usual.

As at Fort George, the officers' privy at Fort Charlotte was flushed with water. This was far different than the privy for the other men and the NCOs. Their privy was located near the shoreline behind their barracks. Harbour tides did the rest. Zachary preferred not to think about those times when he had to use the privy with a cold north wind blowing out of the harbour. For now, the officers' privy had to be dealt with. In a

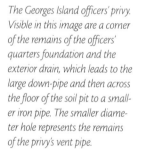

The Georges Island officers' privy. Visible in this image are a corner of the remains of the officers' quarters foundation and the exterior drain, which leads to the large down-pipe and then across the floor of the soil pit to a smaller iron pipe. The smaller diameter hole represents the remains of the privy's vent pipe.

short time, Zachary found the source of the unusually strong smell. To flush the privy, water was collected from the roof of the adjacent officers' quarters and carried to concrete ground-level gutters. At the end of the gutter system, the water flowed into a vertical ceramic pipe that helped to build up its volume before it flowed into the soil pit. The pit needed a good head of water to wash its contents into another pipe that carried the effluent into Halifax harbour. Peering into the pipe, Zachary saw that a partially decayed gull was blocking it.

After removing the gull and clearing the pipe, Zachary walked down the hill for the day's main meal of beef and potatoes. At the barracks, Esther, the artillery sergeant's wife, was unmoved as Zachary poked his head through the open door to say hello. On her hands and knees, she was frantically looking for her crochet needle. Zachary offered to help, but by then Esther realized that the needle had probably fallen through a crack in the wooden floor. (During archaeological excavations at Fort Charlotte, the only artifact recovered that probably belonged to a female was a crochet needle, excavated in 1992 in the area of the sergeants' quarters.) Over dinner, Zachary discussed his morning discovery with Esther's husband Sheldon. From Sheldon he learned that the curved stone feature inside the fort was the remains of the foundation of a Martello Tower that had been built in 1812 and demolished about 1862. The copper nails, Sheldon guessed, had been used to construct the door to the magazine in the bottom floor of the tower. (Copper nails replaced iron nails in any construction where sparks might be created and considered a hazard, especially in a magazine.) After dinner, Zachary's attention turned to the pieces of pottery that had been found near the entrance to the magazine inside the fort. Their decoration was unlike any he had seen before. Esther might be able to help with their identification, but for the moment Zachary was more interested in what Sheldon might know concerning a legend about an underwater tunnel connecting Georges Island and Citadel Hill. (The legend persists to this day, but archaeologists have found no evidence to substantiate it. *That*, however, is another story.)

Plumbing the Past

The fictionalized tales of Zachary Aaron and Bill Alexander could not have been told without the results of numerous archaeological investigations. When archaeologists are diligent, imaginative, and in some cases just plain lucky, they make discoveries that, in a manner of speaking, can bring past human activities back to life. By basing fiction on fact, they have been able to show how, two centuries ago on Citadel Hill and Georges Island, people struggled to solve some of life's most universal, and often unpleasant, challenges to personal hygiene and health.

The Central Trust Affair and Lessons Learned

April D. MacIntyre, Memorial University of Newfoundland
Stephen A. Davis, Saint Mary's University

ARCHAEOLOGICAL SITES ARE NON-RENEWABLE RESOURCES. Once they are gone, they are gone forever. Even so, archaeologists do not automatically oppose development in an effort to keep our underground heritage undisturbed. Development has been part of our past (as reflected in the archaeological record), and it will continue to be a part of our future. It is the loss of underground heritage before it can be properly investigated and documented that archaeologists lament. The story of two archaeological sites in downtown Halifax—discovered almost two decades apart—reveals lessons that were learned, and lessons that can still be learned, about how to protect the underground heritage of the city.

The Salvage of Central Trust

The saga of Central Trust began on a cold, wintry day in early 1984. During the first week of January, a pedestrian walking on Duke Street noticed something peculiar at the site of construction of the new Central Trust (now HSBC) office tower. Amid the mud dredged up by the heavy machinery were fragments of old timbers and artifacts that appeared to be hundreds of years old. The pedestrian reported his observation to the Nova Scotia Museum, and the museum in turn asked an archaeologist to visit the site and assess the situation. By the time the archaeologist appeared at the site, it was clear

Right: John Rocque's plan of Halifax, 1750

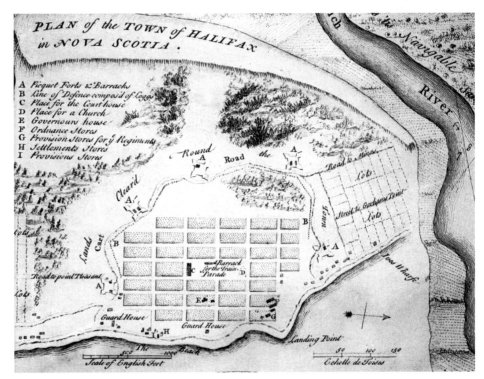

Opposite Page: Archaeology students from Saint Mary's University sift through mounds of fill at the Central Trust landfill site in Prospect, collecting thousands of artifacts from eighteenth-century Halifax.

that much damage had already been done; excavation crews had dug down past the remains of eighteenth- and nineteenth-century buildings. Only a small area at the northeast corner of the block was left undisturbed from the destruction of what—because the site dated back to the founding of Halifax in 1749—was potentially 235 years old.

Within one hour, students salvaged fifteen hundred artifacts from the surface.

Archaeologist Stephen Davis and a crew of students from Saint Mary's University volunteered to salvage the little that was spared. They expanded their effort when they learned that debris from the site had been trucked to a landfill in Prospect. The owners of the landfill, Hill Brothers Construction, allowed a team of twenty-six archaeology students to rescue what artifacts they could from more than a hundred mounds of debris spread over a 0.75-hectare area. Within one hour, the students salvaged fifteen hundred artifacts from the surface; the recovery of artifacts embedded in the mounds would have to wait. In 1984, the protection of archaeological resources threatened with development in Halifax was not a financial responsibility assigned to any one party. Nevertheless, several sources of funding materialized for field and laboratory work. The Summer Canada Works and Environment 2000 program funded the initial phase of field recovery and six weeks of laboratory analysis. Consequently, in the summer of

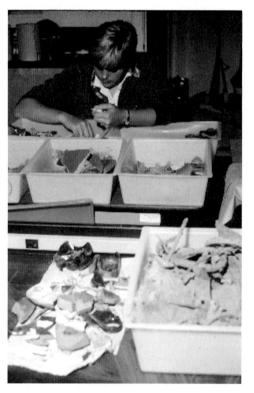

Saint Mary's University student Barbara Bishop sorts and mends artifacts collected from the Central Trust landfill site in Prospect.

1984, Saint Mary's University students returned to the landfill and recovered an additional twenty-five thousand artifacts. The Atlantic Regional Office of Parks Canada assisted in the conservation of recovered iron and organic material, and Manufacturer's Life Insurance Company (owners of the Central Trust Tower) helped fund the preservation of hundreds of recovered leather shoes.

Most of the artifact analysis was carried out in 1985 at Saint Mary's University and funded by the city of Halifax and a federal government employment program called Challenge '85. Seven students worked for four months sorting, mending, and analyzing the artifacts, some of which are now on permanent public display at the Nova Scotia Museum of Natural History.

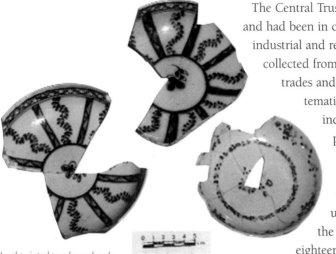

The Central Trust site was part of the original 1749 Halifax town and had been in continuous use for 235 years, serving a variety of industrial and residential functions. Through analysis, the artifacts collected from the site could be linked to various commercial trades and domestic activities; however, due to the unsystematic nature of salvage, they could not be linked to individual buildings. Therefore, their value for interpreting the social history of the site was limited. Unless artifacts can be recovered *in situ* (in their original location) they cannot be reliably related to other artifacts, to the places where they were used, or to the people who used them. Although the site produced what is likely the best collection of eighteenth-century artifacts in Halifax, the loss of their undisturbed archaeological context is unquestionably the most significant consequence of the salvage operation.

Hand-painted pearlware bowls collected from the Central Trust landfill site, dating from the late eighteenth to early nineteenth centuries. These were relatively inexpensive wares, produced mainly in England for export to North America.

The Central Trust affair attracted municipal, provincial, and national media attention. The actions of the developer came under close scrutiny, with newspaper headlines proclaiming, "Workers uncover major archaeological find: Will it be saved?" and "Back to work after rubble-rousing finds: Artifacts recovered, but historic site lost at Central Trust Building dig."

Learning from Central Trust

In 2001, seventeen years after the Central Trust affair, the Halifax Regional Municipality called for an archaeological investigation in advance of construction of a new municipal parkade on the city block bounded by Granville, Hollis, Sackville, and Salter streets. This block had also been part of the original 1749 Halifax town, and throughout the nineteenth and twentieth centuries it was home to many families and businesses. During the late-twentieth century, much of it was bulldozed, levelled, and in-filled, and new buildings were erected atop old ones. However, vestiges of these old buildings—and their associated barns, privies, and garbage dumps—remained for archaeologists to rescue. What was achieved here, in contrast to what was lost at Central Trust, provides a model for future cooperation between urban archaeologists and developers.

Prior to construction of the parkade, archaeologists compiled a detailed land-use and occupancy history of the site. They learned that as early as 1755 it contained no fewer than five structures; three of these were likely residental, while the remaining two, located at the south end of the site, may have been related to Horsman's Fort. Part of the early fortifications surrounding Halifax, Horsman's Fort was located at what is now the northwest corner of the Maritime Centre, at Barrington and Salter streets. By 1784, the fort had been demolished, as had the two associated structures; furthermore, only one of the other three early structures on the site was still standing. By the nineteenth century, the cultural landscape of the site had changed dramatically. Between 1868 and 1895, twenty-eight families and businesses set up stakes there. Granville Street was the busiest area, with several dwellings, privies, and stables, as well as a boarding house, restaurant, and butcher shop. In the course of the twentieth century, the properties changed hands several times until the last remaining buildings were demolished in 1997.

Excavation of the Halifax Regional Municipality parkade site in 2001. The building in the background occupies the site of eighteenth-century Horsman's Fort.

Unlike at Central Trust, archaeologists were in close contact with the developer, and were present at the parkade site from the first phase of ground disturbance and during each subsequent phase of work. In 1997, prior to demolition of the last remaining buildings, the developer asked archaeologists to inspect the basements of these buildings for evidence of any remains, such as wells or privies. During demolition, archaeologists were present to ensure that no archaeological features were destroyed without first being investigated. After demolition, archaeologists were asked to investigate the parking spaces of the old parkade before they too were disturbed. At this time, several artifacts were collected, while the unearthed remains of a wooden structure and scattered building rubble implied that other buildings or related features might lie buried nearby.

A polychrome pearlware plate, collected in 2001 from a mid-nineteenth-century midden at the Halifax Regional Municipality parkade site. The back of the plate bears the distributor's mark "B. O'Neill. 23 Bedford Row, Halifax."

In the winter of 2001, before construction of the parkade began, archaeologists returned to the site to investigate the centre of the block and monitor a crew conducting soil tests. At this time, they discovered a privy and midden (or refuse heap) near Salter Street. Later that spring, archaeologists returned to the site for one last three-week excavation on its west side, along Granville Street. While a crew of five archaeologists worked in conjunction with backhoes, mechanical excavation was limited to the removal of fill deposited during the 1997 demolitions. Twenty additional features were investigated with shovels, rakes, hoes, and trowels.

Altogether, archaeologists collected a total of some 7,700 artifacts at the parkade site between 1997 and 2001, including ceramic sherds, bottle fragments, clay pipes, clay marbles, nails, and buttons. Among the most interesting artifacts were a cannonball and bocce ball. A selection of these artifacts was subsequently exhibited at Halifax Municipal Hall and at the Patrick Power Library at Saint Mary's University.

The archaeological study at the parkade site was widely publicized in the media, but this time—unlike at Central Trust—the publicity was overwhelmingly favourable, with one newspaper headline reporting "Artifacts divulge story of individuals, culture." This favourable publicity reflected the planned cooperation among all interested parties. Because the site was identified in advance as archaeologically significant, developers and archaeologists were able to meet early and plan a course of action to protect the site until it could be investigated. Municipal police even monitored the location in an effort to prevent illegal bottle collectors (frequent trespassers on archaeology sites) from compromising its integrity. Historical research prior to excavation was able to link the recovered artifacts to specific families whose occupations and socioeconomic status became known. Used in conjunction with the artifacts, this information provided tangible evidence of the typical household items of everyday people in nineteenth-century Halifax.

Some of the most interesting insights gained from the careful excavation of the parkade site pertain to nineteenth-century public health and diet. Recovered medicinal bottles and jars of ointments claiming to treat a combination of rheumatism, gout, and "inveterate ulcers, sore breasts, sore head, bad legs, etc." attest to common nineteenth-century ailments and medical treatments. Meanwhile, soil collected from privies yielded seeds and parasitic remains, which, when studied further, will shed light on food preferences and hygiene.

Holloway's ointment jars, collected in 2001 from a mid-nineteenth-century midden at the Halifax Regional Municipality parkade site.

Two Decades of Progress

Support for archaeology is greatest when the public feels a direct connection to the resources that will either be preserved or lost. Since the Central Trust affair, there has been greater emphasis on "public archaeology;" in other words, the involvement of the public in the protection of their underground heritage. In the case of the parkade, this approach was clearly a success. Archaeology in Halifax should now move towards developing programs through which the public can visit and even participate in archaeological excavations and laboratory work.

In Europe, public archaeology programs are long-standing, and in some cases, have resulted in artifacts and portions of old buildings being preserved in innovative ways. For instance, in York, England, when archaeologists discovered the remains of wooden Viking houses during construction of a shopping centre, the centre then incorporated the remains into its basement. The public can now visit the basement and exhibition, and a portion of retail sales revenue from the centre is used to fund a public archaeology program.

As the pace of development in Halifax continues to accelerate, there is an urgent need for public archaeology initiatives of this sort. The magnitude of what was lost at the Central Trust site helped direct attention towards archaeology in the city, leading to concrete changes in the development process. Though there is still much progress to be made in protecting archaeological sites, public archaeology is something that appeals to people of all ages and walks of life. With a little imagination, such popularity could be shaped into a rich, lasting appreciation of Halifax's underground heritage.

ARCHAEOLOGY IN HALIFAX, THEN AND NOW In 1984, when the Central Trust site came to light, there were no municipal regulations stipulating when, where, or how archaeology in Halifax ought to be undertaken. The only regulations were provincial, and they were brought to bear at the last minute by an ad hoc coalition of conscientious citizens, government officials, and business leaders.

Since 1984, much about archaeology in Halifax has changed for the better. There have been more than two hundred archaeology projects in the amalgamated municipality, all of which have raised the profile of archaeology and made it a more accepted part of planning for development. But the regulatory framework remains much the same, and the municipality still lacks a by-law or municipal office dedicated to leading and coordinating archaeological activities.

Halifax has much room to expand the protection and showcasing of its rich archaeological heritage. Municipalities around the world have enshrined archaeology as an obligatory part of urban development and encouraged new developments to incorporate archaeological features on their sites. Many municipalities promote archaeology as an attraction for tourists, sponsor their own archaeological excavations, and support their own archaeology museums. Hopefully, Halifax will follow these examples. –PE

Samuel Sellon's Grandmother's House

Dawn T. Erickson, Erickson's Research Limited

BECAUSE ARCHAEOLOGY IN HALIFAX had always been of the "salvage" sort, in 1986, anthropologist Paul Erickson of Saint Mary's University decided to demonstrate how a knowledge of history could aid in the location of archaeological resources. This was not a new concept; "premeditated" archival research had been used in locating archaeological sites for centuries, quite regularly, all over the world—but not in Halifax. Erickson believed that premeditated research was essential to archaeology, and he wanted to show that sources were available in Halifax to develop historical profiles of sites so that assessments could be made of potential archaeological resources.

The local archaeological community had been shocked in January 1984 by the Central Trust affair, in which an incredibly rich archaeological site was destroyed by heavy construction machinery (see page 18 for details). Despite a brief work stoppage, during which time Saint Mary's students, under the supervision of Stephen Davis, salvaged what they could, nothing could be retrieved in context. For archaeologists, context is essential in interpreting past human events on a site; indeed, it is so invaluable, no site can be properly interpreted without it. This had been a waterfront site when Halifax was founded in 1749. If the more than twenty-five thousand eighteenth-century artifacts ultimately recovered had been retrieved in context, an exciting new view of Halifax could have emerged. The artifacts themselves could have provided a database by which finds elsewhere in the city could have been measured. But by January 1984, it was too late. So much opportunity was lost. Such is "salvage" archaeology.

The Research

This dramatic and archaeologically tragic event caused at least two separate parties to review the situation. The first was A.W. (Dooley) Churchill, then the Heritage Coordinator for the City of Halifax. He hired Nicola Hubbard, a Saint Mary's graduate recently returned from her post-graduate studies at Oxford University, to compile an inventory of potential archaeological sites in Halifax and make recommendations for the future. Churchill retired shortly after Hubbard completed her work, and the initiative ended there.

The other party was Paul Erickson. His objective was to see how effective premeditated archival research could be in locating archaeological sites in Halifax. Erickson began by choosing an area to explore. He chose a site at the southwest corner of Barrington and Cornwallis streets specifically because it was city-owned, vacant land. The site was identified on the land grants map of 1752 as Lot 11 of Section A in the old North Suburbs. It had been granted to Ebenezer Fales. Erickson enlisted me (I was Dawn Mitchell then), a Saint Mary's graduate, to help with the work at the Public Archives of Nova Scotia (now known as Nova Scotia Archives and Records Management, or NSARM). We began to piece together a history of the site, beginning with a study of

Previous page: View of the North Suburbs of Halifax, 1786.

The 1784 Blaskowitz plan of Halifax. A rectangular structure marks Samuel Sellon's grandmother's house.

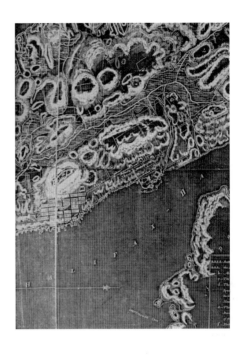

all the early maps they could find. Then we conducted a title-search of the property to determine the chain of ownership. Once the chain of ownership was known, each individual owner was investigated historically.

Erickson and I located two documents that clearly showed a rectangular building on the site: the Blaskowitz 1784 Plan of Halifax and a 1786 watercolour sketch of the Royal Naval dockyard. The building, with its gambrel roof, appeared to be one of the Dutch cottages built in the North Suburbs during that time period. A few of those Dutch cottages were still standing in the twentieth century. One of them was located just one block west of the site and was photographed in 1929. Its foundation appears to measure approximately six by eight metres.

In the course of investigating the individuals who had owned the land, we hit pay dirt. We found a petition to the Crown by Samuel Sellon, dated March 6, 1788. Sellon was petitioning for ownership of the land that had originally been granted to Ebenezer Fales in 1752. In the petition, he stated that the house his grandmother had lived in on the property for at least fifteen years had burned in the fall of 1787. The Crown responded to the petition by escheating, or reclaiming, the land and regranting it to Sellon on the grounds that Fales had not lived in Nova Scotia for at least seven years and had not developed the lot as

This North Suburbs Dutch cottage from 1929 was located one block west of the Sellon site. Its dimensions match those of the structure marked on the 1784 Blaskowitz plan.

the original terms of the grant had stated. The burning of the house was an archaeological stroke of luck. The heavy charcoal layer formed by the burning of the structure would remain even after the passage of the intervening two hundred years. Finding the charcoal layer with associated eighteenth-century artifacts would indicate the location of Samuel Sellon's grandmother's house, and, in turn, finding the remains of Samuel Sellon's grandmother's house would demonstrate the usefulness of premeditated archival research.

The Excavation

The next steps were to assemble an experienced volunteer crew, approach the City of Halifax to obtain permission to use the site for the experiment, and then approach the Nova Scotia Museum to obtain a permit for a preliminary excavation.

I was the first to volunteer; I agreed to help direct the dig with Nicola Hubbard (Hubbard subsequently acted only as consultant). Next came Katie Cottreau and Laird Niven. They had analyzed the artifacts from the Central Trust site, so their help would be invaluable in the interpretation of the artifacts retrieved from the new site. Other volunteers included Paul Erickson, Joseph Tramble and Barbara Bishop.

With archival background research completed and the crew assembled, it was possible to obtain the necessary permission and permit. A. W. (Dooley) Churchill, already committed to planned archaeology, gave the city's blessing. Robert Ogilvie of the Special Places division of the Nova Scotia Museum granted a two-week permit. The work was conducted between May 17 and June 1, 1986, on the site now referred to as the Sellon Site, officially designated BdCv-7.

Conducting archaeology in an urban environment can be distracting, to say the least. In this instance, distractions included cars and trucks speeding by on two sides of the site, a mechanical billboard changing its message every eight seconds—click, click, click—passersby striding along an existing well-trodden path, wanting to know if any "treasure" had been found yet, and reporters wondering what archaeologists wear when they excavate!

Using the *Goad's Insurance Plan* of 1895 as a guide, measurements were made from the middle of Cornwallis and Barrington streets, and a stake was driven into the ground to indicate the area where the five-by-five-metre grid would be laid out for the excavation. The grid, hopefully, would overlay the remains of Samuel Sellon's grandmother's house. Eventually, eighteen pits, each one metre square, were excavated to various depths.

Saint Mary's archaeologist Michael Deal brought his summer school class to the site, and they conducted a survey, which included the mapping of the entire area. This exercise was advantageous for the project and gave hands-on experience to the students. Next, an initial surface-collection took place. Then the sod layer was removed from the entire grid area. It yielded a variety of eighteenth-, nineteenth-, and twentieth-century ceramics, some pipe stems, various metal objects, and pieces of glass. This array of artifacts indicated a good deal of site disturbance. A neighbour revealed that the area had been used as a dumping ground for earth removed from the Uniacke Square housing project on Gottingen Street in the 1960s. This circumstance was not a problem for the archaeological objective, because what was being sought was hidden well underground, but it did explain the jumble of artifacts on and just under the surface.

This view of the Sellon site, taken in 1986, looks westward from Barrington Street. The cottage of Thomas Beamish Akins is visible in the background on the left.

This view looking northward shows red-hued remnants of the brick-lined chimney and the pulverized, grey, mortared area.

With great care, we excavated the pits one by one. Photographs were taken of artifacts as they lay *in situ* (in their original location). Then they were bagged and recorded. The appearance of "sterile" soil, or soil with no evidence of human activity, at a shallow level on the southwest part of the grid was odd. Reaching sterile soil generally means that there is no need to go any deeper. But the Sellon site was in an urban environment, and urban areas are more likely to experience disturbances of various kinds. Perhaps there would be an explanation for the unusual location of this sterile soil when the excavation was complete and all the evidence was gathered. The crew forged on.

After a few days and many anxious moments when we wondered whether we were working in the correct area, Laird Niven exposed what turned out to be part of a foundation wall. The wall was built of slate and quartzite, two rows wide and three courses high. No mortar could be seen. More pits were opened up, following the wall south and west. The interior face of the foundation wall had a finished surface, while the exterior was unfinished.

At the western end of the exposed foundation was a heavily mortared feature, also made of quartzite and slate rocks, but these rocks were red-hued and fire-cracked. Among the mortared rocks were whole and broken red bricks, indicating a brick-lined chimney. As the excavation of this feature progressed, a large number of Buckleyware storage jar sherds was found, as was a flatiron with its handle missing. The Buckleyware dated from the third quarter of the eighteenth century. These finds were exciting, but the biggest reward for us was finding a heavy charcoal layer inside the foundation. Embedded in it and under it were exclusively eighteenth-century artifacts. Hello, Samuel Sellon's grandmother's house!

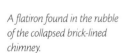

A flatiron found in the rubble of the collapsed brick-lined chimney.

The Interpretation

The stratigraphy (the order and position of different strata) of a site tells its story. The stratigraphy comprises different layers that need to be interpreted in the correct sequence to explain the activities that have taken place there. The layers represent human activity and processes of natural soil formation. Twelve such layers, or "stratigraphic events," were uncovered during the excavation. They were numbered consecutively as they were encountered. The "events" inside the foundation—levels four, six and seven—differed from the "events" outside the foundation—levels eight, nine, ten, and eleven. The foundation wall and the chimney/hearth complex were designated levels five and twelve respectively. The levels require further comment.

Level one, the sod development layer, covered the entire excavation area. This was the layer that contained the great assortment of artifacts from the eighteenth, nineteenth, and twentieth centuries, mentioned earlier. This assemblage was to be expected, given its origin in earth dumped there from elsewhere.

Level two was a mixture of soil, artifacts of the sort found in level one, and rubble.

Level three, the sterile soil that was found in the southwestern section of the excavation area, was orange and yellow with flecks of charcoal and rocks. It was the only level encountered that contained no artifacts. The explanation for its presence so close to the surface was obvious once its proximity to the foundation was established. When the hole was being dug for the foundation in the eighteenth century, some of the sterile soil from its deeper level, level seven, was shoveled up to the surface and deposited there. The flecks of charcoal would have resulted from the spewing out of charcoal as the building collapsed.

Level four was inside the foundation and was a combination of brown organic soil, quartzite, brick, and slate. It contained only a few eighteenth- and nineteenth-century artifacts. This was an interesting layer because the large rocks were uniform in size and oriented in an east-west direction. Because this layer was found only inside the foundation, it appeared that level four was the material used to carefully fill in the foundation after the building had been razed. Why such care was taken with the rocks remains a mystery. The absence of twentieth-century artifacts in this level implies that the foundation was filled in no later than the nineteenth century.

Level six, the heavy charcoal layer, was found only inside the foundation. It was the first layer to contain only eighteenth-century artifacts. Pieces of burned planks, some with nails embedded in them, were found in this layer. All of the nails recovered were hand-wrought, roseheaded nails, the kind used in the eighteenth century until the more modern machine-cut nails started to be produced around 1790. The type of ceramics, pipe bowls, pipe stems, and bottle fragments found all confirmed the eighteenth-century context. Two gunspalls, or pieces of flint used to ignite rifle fire, were found under the level six charcoal layer, and both dated to the eighteenth century.

The occurrence of the heavy charcoal layer only inside the foundation is consistent with the way a burning structure collapses: burned material collapses inward. Residual accumulation occurs outside the structure due to the spewing of some of the burned material at the moment of collapse. The charcoal-flecking found in levels three and

The finished excavation reveals the southeast section of the foundation, the collapsed chimney hearth area, and the filled-in interior.

nine—at the same depth—was probably the residual accumulation deposited when the structure collapsed. Possibly the thin charcoal line, level eight, was also deposited at that moment.

Level seven, found inside the foundation, was the same orange and yellow sterile soil as in level three. Level seven appeared to be the tamped base preparation for the house construction, and, like level six, yielded only eighteenth-century artifacts. Levels eight, nine, ten, and eleven were found outside the foundation.

The artifacts recovered from the site and the soil/event levels provided by the stratigraphy gave a good chronology of the site even in this preliminary excavation. The deepest levels, six and seven, yielded only eighteenth-century artifacts. Level six, with its associated artifacts, proved the structure had burned down in the last quarter of the eighteenth century. Level four, with its eighteenth-century and a few nineteenth-century artifacts mixed in, proved that the foundation was filled in after the structure burned down.

The main purpose of this excavation was to find the remains of Samuel Sellon's grandmother's house that had burned in the fall of 1787. The assemblage of artifacts suggested a domestic site. Level six provided evidence of a fire. The artifacts associated with the burn layer and the hearth suggested the time of the fire—circa 1787. Even the dimensions of the foundation wall and chimney and hearth complex were in keeping with the dimensions and design of a North Suburbs Dutch cottage. Nothing was found in the course of the excavation to contradict the probability that Samuel Sellon's grandmother's house had been located. The crew had demonstrated that the archival sources in Halifax could be sufficient to predict the location of archaeological resources.

SAMUEL SELLON'S GRANDMOTHER The reader might be curious about the identity of Samuel Sellon's grandmother. After the archaeology project was over, I conducted extensive genealogical research on the Sellon family. I was able to compile most of the genealogy from their arrival in Halifax on the first ships in 1749 down to the present day. Unfortunately, I found no information about the name or personal circumstances of Samuel's grandmother. The grandmother will have to remain largely anonymous for now. –DE

The Aftermath

The excavation attracted a great deal of media attention. Radio, television and newspaper reporters gave enthusiastic coverage, and the site even made the national television news. A joke made by the excavation director regarding the number of pipe-bowls and stems found on the site resulted in a newspaper story suggesting that the house burned down because someone was smoking in bed. (Lesson learned: never joke with a newspaper reporter!)

Since 1986, circumstances have changed considerably for archaeology in Halifax. Much more consultation now takes place. Archaeology has become a more accepted and expected part of development. Archival research and title-searches are regularly part of archaeological assessments of sites. Those who were involved with finding the remains of Samuel Sellon's grandmother's house would like to think that they helped in some way to raise the profile of archaeology and bring about these changes. The truth is, every archaeologist who has worked on a site in Halifax has helped to raise the profile of archaeology. Raising that profile is important, because it shows how much archaeologists can contribute to unearthing the urban past that awaits discovery just beneath ground.

The crew in 1986. Seated from left to right are Katie Cottreau, Laird Niven, Dawn Mitchell, Joseph Tramble, Barbara Bishop, and Paul Erickson.

Avoiding the Bulldozer

Archival Resources for Archaeology Downtown

Liam D. Murphy, California State University, Sacramento

N THE EARLY 1990s, THE MEMORY OF WHAT HAD BEEN lost in the Central Trust affair of 1984 (see page 18 for details) was still fresh. Clearly, what might have been a project of tremendous archaeological significance had been reduced to a salvage operation. For Halifax's small yet active community of archaeologists and local historians, the incident raised the distressing possibility of future irrecoverable losses to the city's historical heritage. Alarmingly, future episodes of this type seemed likely, if not inevitable, given the *fait accompli* of ongoing development in the municipality. When speaking to the international conference Doing Urban Archaeology (hosted by the Nova Scotia Archaeology Society in 1989), Robert Stapells—at that time a prominent developer and advocate for the preservation of valuable archaeological resources—conceded as much in referring to downtown Halifax as "the most expensive real estate in eastern Canada."

However, there existed one clear lesson to emerge from the Central Trust incident upon which everyone—scientists, urban planners, developers, and politicians, among others—could agree: that it might all have been avoided had there been a means of anticipating the presence of archaeological sites in the metropolitan area. In 1992, after discussing a number of options with my Saint Mary's University honours thesis supervisor, anthropologist Paul Erickson, I decided to try to address this issue. The plan was to develop a comprehensive archaeological resource inventory for a well-defined, and currently undeveloped, property somewhere in the core of Halifax's historic downtown. Making use of all available primary and secondary resources (including title deeds, fire insurance plans, "bird's eye view" sketches, and popular histories of the city), the project's goal was to assemble a chronology of land use on the site, which would make it possible to predict the nature, scope, and importance of archaeological materials that might be present, should the site eventually face redevelopment.

Below: This view of the upper level of the study area from the corner of Sackville and Market streets shows the Halifax Herald *parking lot on Grafton Street. In the background are the Midtown Tavern and some high-rise buildings.*

Previous page: This 1787 lease describes a house to be built on the corner of Grafton and Sackville streets.

Six Lots on Market, Sackville, and Grafton Streets

Selected for the study were six property lots that straddle an unassuming downtown city block, conspicuous only for being underdeveloped. Bordered on three sides by Market (or Albermarle, until it was rechristened in 1917), Sackville, and Grafton streets, these lots represent roughly one-third of the block (Prince Street, which runs along the block's far end, borders properties not included in this study). The lots are positioned on two adjacent plateaus on the otherwise steep descent toward Halifax Harbour. Separated from each other by a concrete and gravel retaining wall, one plateau abuts Market Street on the block's hill side, while the other faces Grafton Street below. The location of these lots within the downtown core makes them not only an attractive target for development (in 2004, nearly the entire block was a gravel parking lot), but also the possible resting place of cultural artifacts from the city's earliest days.

At the founding of Halifax in 1749, this block, like those around it, was parcelled into two parallel rows of eight lots each. Correspondence from John Bruce and Charles Morris (respectively, the settlement expedition's engineer and surveyor) to the British Board of Trade and Plantations reveals how the land was plotted. The old town's blocks were designed to be 320 feet (97.6 metres) long by 120 feet (36.6 metres) deep, and were subdivided into sixteen lots, each measuring 40 by 60 feet (12.1 by 18.3 metres). When compared to a land registration map from the early 1990s, the town's original "Allotment Book" (a record of the first land grants made by the Crown to settlers in 1749) confirms that despite more than 250 years of urban development, the streets of Halifax's historic core, including the six lots in question, have largely retained their original dimensions.

It is recorded that by their first winter, in 1749, Halifax's colonists had built about 350 dwellings on the forty or so blocks bounded by the town's wooden palisade wall. However, details of the initial development of the study site are not known. Most primary documentation of early architecture in eighteenth-century Halifax provides little more than anecdotal evidence about the presence of buildings on the site, much less the economic and social activities taking place there. For instance, neither a 1755 French map of Halifax (designed in preparation for a possible invasion) nor a 1764 sketch drawn from Georges Island do more than merely suggest the presence of four or five structures straddling the six lots. Certainly, these structures would have been modest. Halifax historian Thomas Raddall drew upon various official descriptions in characterizing the town's early dwellings as "long huts...sheathed with boards" in the midst of streets "still rough with stones and old tree stumps." In subsequent years, many of these inelegant dwellings would be replaced by "frame houses built on low foundations of dry stone wrenched from the hillside" (Raddall, 42).

Deeds, Licenses, and Contracts (1749–1869)

While it is difficult to know the extent to which documents like bird's-eye view sketches accurately reflect eighteenth-century architectural detail, title deeds provide a reliable picture of the ownership of downtown properties during the period. Between 1749 and 1800, these deeds reveal owners of the lots on the study site to have included carpenters, traders, mariners, merchants, at least one tailor, at least one fisherman, at least one soldier, and at least one tavern owner. Given the limited amount of housing available in the early town, it seems likely that at least some of these business activities were conducted out of the homes of residents. Again we may turn to Raddall, who describes typical eighteenth-

Harry Jackson's 1945 map of Halifax. Jackson created this map, which identifies original property owners in the study area, based on records from the town's original allotment book. Sackville Street runs along the top, with parallel Prince Street below it, bordering Saint Paul's Church.

Left: This 1755 document licensed the Union Flag, one of two early taverns on Albermarle (now Market) Street.

Right: This 1755 document licensed the Bottle and Glass, one of two early taverns on Albermarle (now Market) Street.

century Halifax shops as "small and crude, most of them simply a front room in a dwelling, with goods exposed on a broad shutter let down on hinges in the day and closed up at night" (42).

Among the known business activities associated with the early years of the site was the selling of alcohol. Robert Douglas was the owner of two lots on Albermarle Street from 1752 to 1758, and although his occupation is not spelled out in any of the early title deeds, he is named on a pair of licenses as being the proprietor of two Halifax drinking establishments (surely among the town's earliest). It would seem that the two "grog" houses were located side by side on Albermarle Street. Dated September and December 1755, the licenses constitute contracts between Douglas (and business associates) and the lieutenant-governor of Nova Scotia for the legal establishment of two taverns, which appear to have been called The Union Flag and The Bottle and Glass. The proliferation of drinking establishments in early colonial Halifax—particularly in this part of town—would earn the so-called "upper streets" a certain infamy in the years to come. One newcomer is cited by Raddall as writing to an American friend that "there are 1,000 houses in the town. We have upwards of 100 licensed [drinking] houses and perhaps as many without license, so the business of one half of the town is to sell rum and the other half to drink it" (65). Indeed, historian Judith Fingard has discussed how the debauched reputation of the upper streets grew unabated throughout the nineteenth century. Notorious for their taverns, brothels, and teeming population of

DOWN AND OUT ON THE UPPER STREETS Halifax's nightlife is not what it used to be. Within the space of a few blocks, Barrack, Albermarle and Grafton streets in the late eighteenth and nineteenth centuries offered an array of taverns and brothels catering to the lewdest and most dissolute behaviour. It was a part of town that a respectable woman would avoid, and where, after dark, a gentleman feared for his safety. Indeed, the evil reputation of these upper streets was such that military authorities eventually ruled them out of bounds to soldiers, though the effectiveness of this ban can be questioned. Barrack Street—positioned at the foot of the harbour slope of Citadel Hill—was, as its name suggests, the site of quarters for regiments stationed in Halifax. That so much sin so nearby presented a powerful temptation is evident in records of soldiers admitted to military hospital after flaunting the ban (whether for injuries from drunken brawls or due to venereal disease it is not clear). Only the success of the temperance movement, which brought prohibition to Halifax in 1916, changed the character of the upper streets. And in an attempt to shed their sordid past, the street names were changed: Barrack Street became part of Brunswick, while Albermarle was renamed Market. –RP transient labour and mariners, they were havens, as she phrases it, for "the destitute, drunken, and dependent" (Fingard, 17–19).

Some thirty years later, in 1787, another of Robert Douglas's properties (located at the intersection of Grafton and Sackville streets) was the subject of a different sort of contract: a document of lease between its new owner, James Pedley, trader, and John Draddy, carpenter. This stipulates that Draddy agrees "to Build upon the above recited Lot One Substantial Framed House to be at least Twenty five Feet Long and Eighteen Feet Wide with good and Sufficient Chimneys and fire places in said House" (NSARM 1787). Curiously, a second lease was drawn the following year between Draddy and another carpenter, Lawrence Fearney. In this second contract, Fearney agrees to build a dwelling of slightly different dimensions: "The said Lawrence Fearney…doth covenant himself…unto the said John Drad[d]y…to build upon the above recited lot one house eighteen feet long by fifteen feet broad with one story high & a good and sufficient chimney" (Nova Scotia Registry of Deeds 1788). In the absence of further documentation, the circumstances surrounding these contracts cannot be known for certain. Perhaps Draddy, unable to undertake the work himself, had simply subcontracted the construction of James Pedley's house. However, the other possibility, suggested by the discrepancy in dimensions, is that the second contract is evidence of another house being built on the same property. Either way, these documents attest to the continued development of the study site toward the end of the eighteenth century.

During the first half of the nineteenth century, property owners on the block seem to have struck a balance between commercial and residential activity. Over the course of these decades, lot owners included craftsmen, such as tailors and blacksmiths, and small entrepreneurs, such as furriers and grocers—although the degree to which these trades were pursued on the properties themselves remains an open question. Unhappily, where eighteenth-century title deeds frequently specify the professional occupations of lot owners, nineteenth-century documentation tends to be less precise. For example, many nineteenth-century deeds refer instead to a given proprietor's social title, such as "gentleman"; general occupation, such as "esquire" or "merchant"; or military rank, such as "yeoman" or "militia staff sergeant."

The Advent of Modern Documentation (1869–1980)

While in some respects less "exciting" from an antiquarian's perspective, land use in downtown Halifax during the second half of the nineteenth century proves much easier to document. In particular, publication of the first city directory in 1869 is a watershed for Halifax historians. From this point on, an unbroken record of structures and activities exists for the entire downtown area. This more complete archival resource available

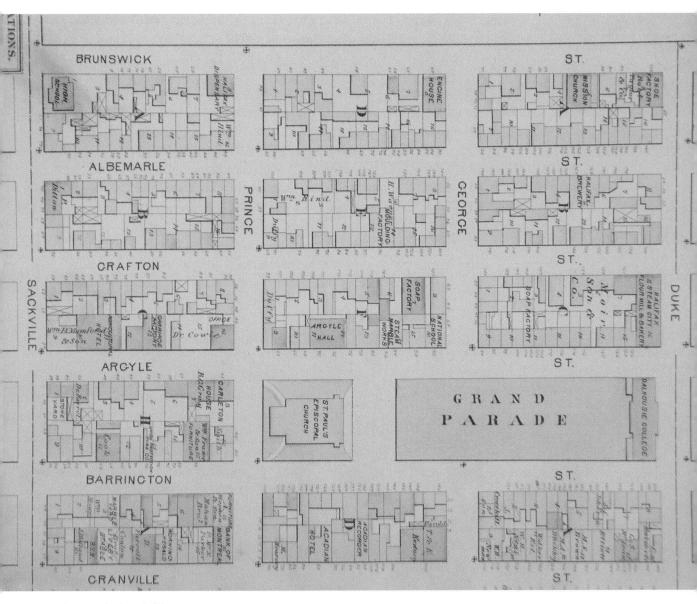

This 1878 atlas shows buildings and other structures in the study area.

to us consists not only of street directories, but also of seven fire insurance plans, a number of building and demolition permits relating to the site, Hopkins's land use atlas of the city published in 1878, and (in later years) photographic documentation.

Between 1863 and 1909, at least one property on the block served as a grocery and liquor store, as well as a residence, and perhaps as the location of a number of other small businesses. A title deed indicates that in 1863 Patrick Dillon, grocer, purchased the lot occupying the corner of Albermarle and Sackville streets. Its subsequent use as a grocery is corroborated by Hopkins's 1878 atlas and several fire insurance plans. City directories indicate that this establishment operated on the property until 1909, after which it seems to have been converted for a brief period of time into a restaurant. While evidence concerning other specific businesses on the study site during the period is less abundant, city directories do suggest the presence of other commercial establishments either adjacent to or within the same structure as the grocery store. These may have included such varied occupations as shoe-making, tailoring, carpentry, butchering, fruit-selling, printing, coopering, harness making, radio servicing, and barbering.

In 1877, city directories establish the introduction of a new element to the history of land use on the site. A blacksmith's forge—located midway between Sackville and Prince streets—brought an industrial presence to the block. In a will drawn up in 1901, John O'Connell bequeathed the forge to his sons, William and Lawrence, who evidently continued to run the business until its sale in 1918.

> I give and bequeath to my sons William J. O'Connell and Lawrence J. O'Connell the building and premises now occupied by me as a Blacksmith's Forge, and known as number forty-two and forty-four Grafton Street in the City of Halifax aforesaid together with the tools and stock in trade contained there, to share and share alike. (Nova Scotia Registry of Deeds 1901)

In 1920, the blacksmith's forge disappeared, to be replaced by an enterprise that would endure for most of the twentieth century. From its inception, Albert Chappell's vulcanizing works and battery electric service (Chappell & Son Ltd.) was a successful venture, and it steadily expanded into neighbouring properties on Grafton and Market streets throughout the mid-twentieth century. During the first nineteen years of the operation's existence, it was characterized by activities such as the manufacture of tires, auto-repair service, and storage. Beginning in 1939, electric service was also incorporated into the business. The operation was of particular importance during World War Two, at which time it served as a base of military repairs and storage.

Another example of property use on the study site in the twentieth century involved Ada J. MacCallum, a notorious brothel keeper. She owned a building at Grafton and Sackville streets in 1955.

Another, more salacious, example of property use on the study site in the twentieth century (one recalling the notoriety of the upper streets from years past) involved Ada J. MacCallum, a notorious brothel keeper. Barring the existence of a second Ada MacCallum—and the lady in question will be remembered as one of a kind by Haligonians of a certain age—a title deed indicates that she enjoyed a brief tenure as owner of a building at the intersection of Grafton and Sackville streets in 1955. This was the same nineteenth-century building owned by the grocer Patrick Dillon many years before. If MacCallum's hope was to run another brothel, the idea seems to have withered on the vine; she sold the property a year after buying it. Less colourfully, perhaps, this building's last commercial use was as a paint supply shop between 1966 and 1977.

City directories establish that other ventures conducted on the block during the later twentieth century included tailoring and upholstering, television and appliance sales and repair, meat sales, and furniture repair. However, later commercial activities were, on the whole, exceptions to how property on the block was used as the twentieth century wore on. City directories suggest a pattern of dwindling activity, with the site becoming increasingly residential (particularly on the second and third floors of buildings) until the properties were eventually vacated.

Demolition and Development (1980–Present)

As described to me by the Halifax Herald Project Management Division in September 2004, prior to their purchase by the Herald, the six lots in question had been owned by and had changed hands among several local development companies. In 1980, the ageing buildings occupying the lots were condemned by the city, after which they remained vacant for a number of years. In 1985, Canterbury Group Ltd. (CGL) purchased all but the northeastern-most properties on the block in separate parcels from Centennial Realities Ltd., John Laba (a merchant), and Battery & Electric Service Ltd. (the corporation that had managed the Chappell & Son business since the early 1950s). Intended for a commercial construction project, the block was razed by CGL in 1986. However, other business opportunities arose, precluding development, and in 1987 CGL sold the properties to Grafton Investments, a subsidiary of the Halifax Herald Ltd., which gravelled them for use as a parking facility for its staff. In April 2002, the lots were sold to another development company, Landmark Development Corporation, which has since voiced its intention to develop the property.

Other ventures conducted on the block in the twentieth century included tailoring and upholstering, television and appliance sales and repair, meat sales, and furniture repair.

Robert Stapells, founder of CGL, offered extensive insight into the 1986 demolition of the buildings on the study site. Consistent with the general practices of urban demolition, a swivel hoe and other machinery (rather than explosives) were employed in razing existing structures on the properties. The immediate goal was to level off, or grade, the site. Prior to demolition, the buildings on the southeastern and northwestern lots of the study area were first stripped of any valuable material that might be easily salvaged: in Stapell's estimation, a motley assortment of artifacts that included doors, doorknobs, sinks, bathtubs, and even some stained glass. This material, much of which dated to the nineteenth century, was saved or sold. Subsequently, the buildings were demolished, their debris pulled into the centre of the site and then collected either for deposition at a

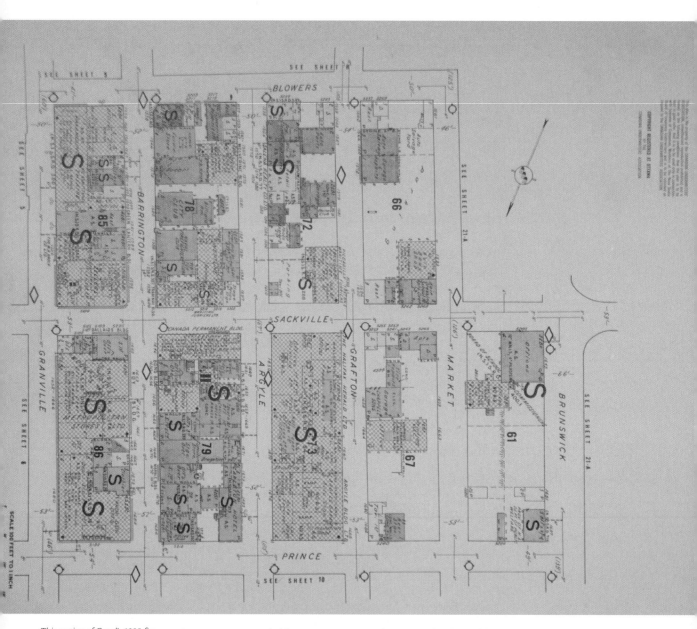

This section of Goad's 1895 fire insurance plan shows the study area in great detail. At the time, the area was past its commercial prime.

dump in Harrietsfield, Nova Scotia, or for use as harbour fill. In contrast to the relative ease with which the two condemned residential and commercial structures were disposed of, the sturdier concrete and steel foundations of the Chappell & Son building required some labour-intensive jackhammering.

Significantly, Robert Stapells's intimate knowledge of the development process drew attention to architectural features that had not been revealed in my documentary search, features which may yet prove invaluable for archaeologists. When Chappell & Son and the neighbouring McCurdy's print shop (which, erected in the early 1950s, straddled several lots between Grafton and Market) were constructed, concrete slabs were poured over their footings in order to lay new foundations. It is therefore possible, if not likely, that two basements predating these buildings were left intact (or at least relatively undisturbed) beneath the concrete. In Stapells's estimation, this time capsule of underground Halifax might well date to the early nineteenth century, if not before. This perspective is supported by the documentary record, which suggests the same building occupied the corner of Albermarle/Market and Sackville streets from at least the mid-nineteenth century until 1980.

Archaeological Potential

As this brief review of land use on one city block suggests, even the most undistinguished vacant lot, dismissed by many as an eyesore or worse, can be a rich cultural resource in historically significant cities like Halifax. Obviously, excavation of the area could greatly contribute to our understanding of everyday life in the eighteenth, nineteenth, and early twentieth centuries. Of particular interest, based on the site usage established by title deeds and leases, are Robert Douglas's taverns on Albermarle Street and James Pedley's "substantial framed house" on the block's Grafton Street side. Were these to be carefully excavated and studied, they would surely open a rare window onto commercial and residential life in the early years of the city. Quite apart from the tantalizing prospect of the concrete-bound, gravel-veiled time capsule alluded to by Robert Stapells, the blacksmith's forge on Market Street bequeathed in John O'Connell's will is a compelling site for archaeological investigation, for the light it might shed on economic activity in Victorian and Edwardian Halifax.

Furthermore, excavation offers the potential for broader insights into the sociology of urban life in Nova Scotia over the course of three centuries. Together with the understanding of the site's history established by the archival record, excavation would give archaeologists, historians, social geographers, and others the opportunity to study how such variables as topography, demography, economic organization, and social heterogeneity and hierarchy contributed to land use and artifact deposition. For instance, the site's transition from one on which tradespeople, shopkeepers, and artisans were active to one largely consumed with industrial activity—with an attendant reduction in residential use—suggests a fundamental transformation in the organization of space in downtown Halifax between the late eighteenth and late nineteenth centuries (to say nothing of broader economic and political transformations underway across eastern Canada and the United States).

Finally, with regard to this particular city block, time might be of the essence if the loss of an archaeological resource on the scale of the Central Trust incident is to be avoided. In July 2004, the Midtown Tavern, which has sat on the corner of Grafton and Prince streets since 1949, received the endorsement of the Halifax Peninsula Community Council for a massive redevelopment project. Since 1986, the modest three-storey Midtown has been the only structure standing on the study block (though, despite its own storied past, it was not included in this land-use inventory). If plans go ahead, the existing Midtown will be replaced with a seventeen-storey hotel complex, including commercial space and an expanded tavern. It seems hard to imagine that a development of this scope would not have some impact on the adjoining properties, or their buried histories. Though demolition of the existing Midtown was original scheduled for fall 2004, protests by heritage protection groups have delayed these plans. In May 2005, the Nova Scotia Utility and Review Board met to hear these groups' concerns that the cumulative effects of high-rise construction such as this will impair the harbour view from Citadel Hill. Whatever the outcome of this hearing, it is clear that the pace of development in Halifax will not leave this block untouched forever. Even if the bulldozer cannot be avoided, it is to be hoped that—for this and other sites in historic Halifax—the archaeological heritage of the city may still be preserved.

For their kind assistance, the author wishes to thank Gary Castle, Dawn Erickson, the Halifax Herald, Marg and Bill McCurdy, Mary Murphy, Patricia Murphy, Robert Stapells, and Garry Shutlak.

What Maps Can Show Us

Danny Dyke, Nova Scotia Museum of Natural History

ONE OF THE DRIVING FORCES behind archaeology in recent years has been the pace of land development. This is certainly true in busy Halifax, a rapidly-growing urban centre. But development can destroy archaeological sites before they have been excavated, creating tension between archaeologists and developers.

Archaeologists prefer to leave sites in the ground, where they have been safely hidden for generations, rather than just dig them to satisfy their own curiosity. They realize that their activity is ultimately destructive—archaeology is like ripping out the pages to read a book. While archaeologists can "read" the book by digging, they also destroy it in the process. Unless all of the read information is carefully recorded, it is lost forever.

Present-day archaeologists' techniques have reached a level of sophistication undreamed of by their predecessors, and future methods will undoubtedly only get better—assuming, of course, that future archaeologists will have anything left to read and record. Therein lies the dilemma: how to reconcile the potentially conflicting desires to preserve sites for future generations, and to develop new living and working space for a growing population? This dilemma has led many archaeologists to adopt a planning approach known as cultural resource management, which seeks to make informed decisions about what should be preserved and what might be sacrificed. Cultural resource managers cannot make educated decisions, however, without knowing whether and where archaeological sites might exist.

The Changed Landscape

The Halifax area has been continuously and intensively inhabited by Europeans since 1749, and undoubtedly it was inhabited, although more sporadically and sparsely, by First Nations people throughout the preceding eleven thousand years. The effect that First Nations inhabitants had on the land was relatively slight; it was the more recent European inhabitants who began to reshape the Halifax landscape extensively.

Most of us presume that we walk upon the same land that our forebears walked upon. But we are mistaken. In the late eighteenth century, if we had walked along the east side of Lower Water Street, we would have had to watch our footing so as not to stumble; we would have been walking on a beach. Today, the Cogswell Street interchange makes it difficult to walk along Barrington Street from Scotia Square to Cornwallis Street, but in the 1760s, we would have easily walked along this route on a path leading from the north town gate. In the 1850s, we would have followed the same route on a roadway skirting the fences of the Ordnance Yard, where all kinds of "modern" naval weapons were stored and repaired.

How do we know this? By studying maps. One of the advantages of having a large military establishment in Halifax is the abundance of high-quality maps that have been created since the founding of the city. By studying these maps, we can learn what used

*Previous page: J. F. DesBarres'
view of Halifax from the
Dartmouth shore, c.1770*

to be in modern locations—and what archaeological sites might lie underfoot. Let us use one of these maps to travel back to 1827.

Halifax in 1827

In 1827, William Moorsom of the 52nd Regiment Light Infantry created an impressive map of Halifax and environs. Let us imagine Moorsom using his own map to guide him from St. Margaret's Bay into town.

As Moorsom approached Geizer's Hill (today marked by the communications tower atop Fairview) he noticed that the road was barely passable in places. He stopped for refreshments at the Bedford Inn near the shoreline of Bedford Basin (today, the site of the inn is filled in for railways and the Fairview container terminal). From the inn, it was a relatively short distance to the Northwest Arm, across an isthmus that the military was keenly interested in protecting. Uphill from the inn near the isthmus, Moorsom saw

William Moorsom's 1827 map of Halifax and environs.

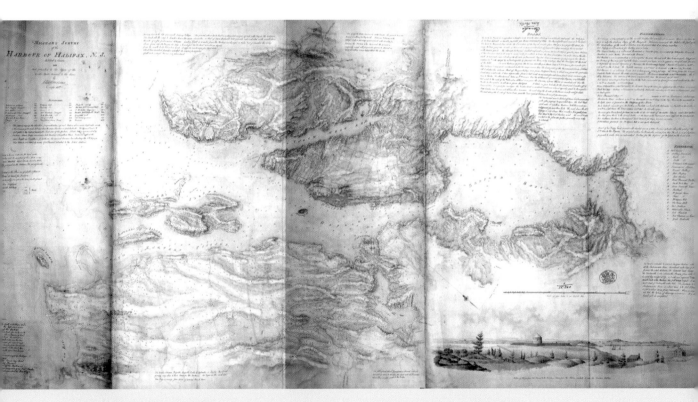

WILLIAM MOORSOM Captain William Scarth Moorsom (1804–1863) holds a special place in Nova Scotia's history. A British captain in the 52nd Regiment Light Infantry, Moorsom was especially perceptive and was fond of writing down his observations and sketches of the colony when stationed in Nova Scotia during the 1820s. His volume, *Letters from Nova Scotia, Comprising Sketches of a Young Country* (London: 1830), is a rare first-hand account of garrison Halifax and the many social customs he witnessed, as well as his intriguing interactions with Nova Scotians. –SM

James Straton's 1796 map of Halifax shows the location of military blockhouses along the peninsular isthmus.

one of the military blockhouses there. If he had consulted an earlier map created by James Straton in 1796, he would have seen the location of the other blockhouses (archivist Harry Piers re-mapped the same locations in 1940).

Continuing into town, Moorsom followed what is now part of Kempt Road. He had a choice of either shifting onto what became Windsor Street and proceeding through a series of farms, or continuing along Kempt until he reached the present-day intersection of Kempt, Young, and Robie streets. Following Robie south would have taken him across the original Halifax Commons, a huge swath of land to the west of town, and swampy land that was the source of a brook. Freshwater Brook still flows today underneath some of the buildings built on the commons.

Moorsom decided instead to follow Young Street towards Halifax Harbour, past the farms along Gottingen Street and old Fort Needham, just north of the intersection of Gottingen and Young. (His map did not show many farms to the north of here, but it did show a road in the vicinity of present-day Richmond Street leading down to the harbour. Today, this site is obliterated by landfill.) Looking at his map more closely, he saw a stream, which, where it entered the harbour, may have been visited by First Nations people, and looking across the harbour toward Dartmouth, he saw a First Nations settlement at Tuft's Cove. Farther south on the Dartmouth shore he caught a glimpse of the red windmill that gave its name to Windmill Road, as well as more farms near where naval ships replenished their supplies of fresh water, at a stream from Albro's Lake to the harbour. If he had consulted Straton's earlier map, he would have seen the location of a nearby old fortification, which by 1827 was only a memory.

William Moorsom's 1827 map with superimposed features, a composite map created by author Danny Dyke. It shows roads in yellow, activity areas in purple, and watercourses in blue.

Looking down the shoreline toward Halifax, Moorsom saw two wharves at the bottom of an extension of Young Street (today, these wharves lie beneath the Halifax Shipyards). To get to the wharves, he had to either walk along the beach or climb up Fort Needham Hill to Gottingen Street. He decided to make the climb and continued south on Gottingen until he reached North Street, passing several more farms along the way. At North, he had a fine view of the Naval Dockyard, which looked much different than it does today. Inside the dockyard he saw only wood and stone buildings, not huge metal-skinned buildings, giant electric cranes, and concrete wharves. All the ships were wooden sailing ships with canvas sails and tall masts, stored in a large pond at the dock-

yard's south end. The streets above the dockyard were lined with buildings; by 1827, Halifax had become a busy place.

Digitizing the Past

Below: J. F. DesBarres' 1778 map of Halifax harbour and peninsula shows landforms, streets, buildings, and wharves.

By accompanying William Moorsom on his imaginary 1827 journey, we can see how his map helps us visualize the present superimposed on the past. But this superimposition is relatively imprecise. Can we make it more accurate?

While studying archaeology at Saint Mary's University, I learned how to georeference and digitize old Halifax maps. Georeferencing uses computer-based Geographical Information Systems (GIS) to relate points on an old map to their real-world geographical positions. Digitizing converts images on the map into computer lines and shapes. The result is a map that can be accurately and conveniently re-scaled and manipulated into a composite with a modern map. The composite can then be used to show the geographical location of old roads and buildings—and potential archaeological sites.

In 2003, I used part of Moorsom's 1827 map to create just such a composite. It was part of an undertaking by the Nova Scotia Museum of Natural History to create a composite map of all Halifax showing zones of high archaeological potential. The image of the composite reproduced on the previous page does not identify the archaeological zones, but it does identify roads in yellow; activity areas such as farms, buildings, and wharves in purple; and watercourses in blue.

Digitizing 1778

Opposite: J. F. DesBarres' map with superimposed digitized features, a composite map created by author Danny Dyke that highlights features along the Halifax waterfront downtown and south of downtown.

I also created another digitized composite map based on a 1778 map of Halifax Harbour by Joseph DesBarres. This composite allows us to see precisely what used to be located along Water Street—and what might still be there to protect, or, if development necessitates, for archaeologists to dig up and record.

In 1778, a stream flowed through the present-day sites of Scotia Square and the Cogswell Street Interchange. Beneath where the interchange ramps are today, and beside the modern Casino Nova Scotia Hotel, used to stand the Five Gun Battery. Just south of

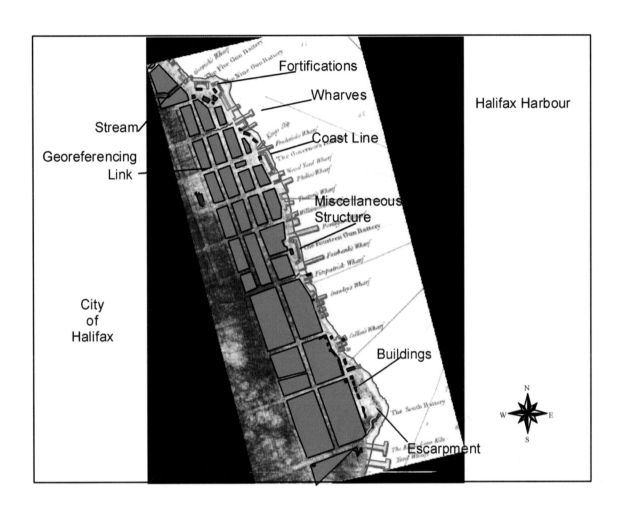

Fortifications

Wharves

Halifax Harbour

Stream

Coast Line

Georeferencing
Link

Miscellaneous
Structure

City
of
Halifax

Buildings

Escarpment

N
W E
S

200   0   200   400 Meters

1778 DesBarres Digitization

#	1778 GeoRef Links		1778 Batteries		1778 Coast Line
	1778 Misc Structures		1778 City Blocks		Escarpment
	1778 Buildings		1778 Wharves		
	1778 Streams		1778 High Water Mark		

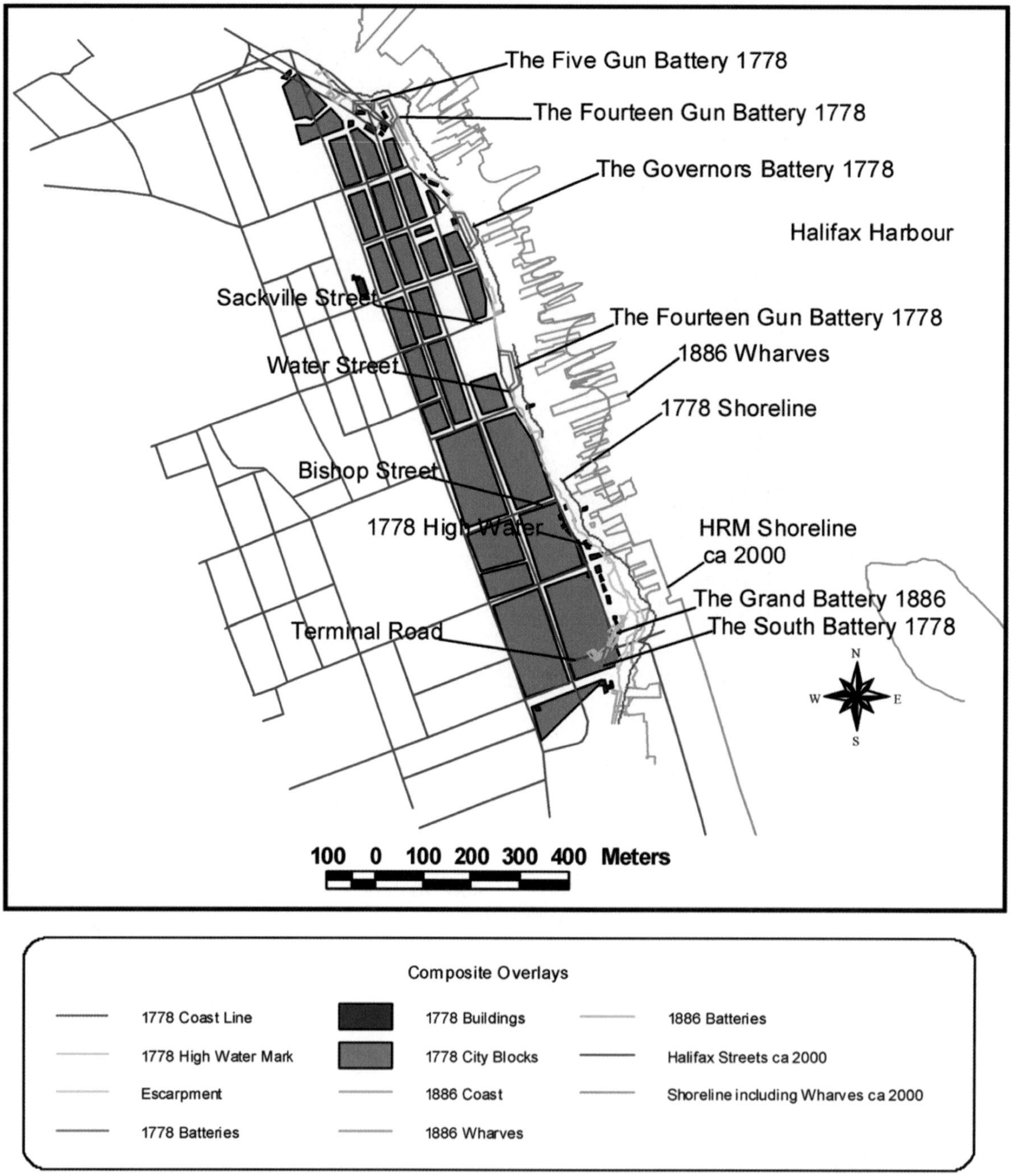

The Five Gun Battery 1778
The Fourteen Gun Battery 1778
The Governors Battery 1778
Halifax Harbour
Sackville Street
The Fourteen Gun Battery 1778
1886 Wharves
Water Street
1778 Shoreline
Bishop Street
1778 High Water
HRM Shoreline ca 2000
The Grand Battery 1886
Terminal Road
The South Battery 1778
N
W
E
S
100 0 100 200 300 400 Meters
Composite Overlays
1778 Coast Line
1778 High Water Mark
Escarpment
1778 Batteries
1778 Buildings
1778 City Blocks
1886 Coast
1886 Wharves
1886 Batteries
Halifax Streets ca 2000
Shoreline including Wharves ca 2000

the battery (between the hotel and Historic Properties) was the Nine Gun Battery. These batteries faced the water, and just behind them, underneath modern Upper Water Street, were six buildings. Another stream crossed Upper Water at Duke Street, and there were more wharves and buildings on the site of the present-day Law Courts. Part of the location of the Governor's Battery now lies beneath Lower Water Street and the parking lots on the street's east side. There were still more wharves and buildings along the east side near the Maritime Museum of the Atlantic. Water Street came by its name honestly—in 1778, the high water mark may have reached the street itself. Water certainly lapped against the Fourteen Gun Battery, on the east side of the street between Sackville and Salter streets.

Yet another stream flowed along Salter Street into the harbour. In this area, the high-water mark almost reached the location of what became Keith's Brewery, and wharves with their associated buildings extended from the shore to most of present-day Bishops Landing (unfortunately, no archaeology took place in advance of the Bishops Landing construction). South of Bishop and Morris streets there were more buildings along Lower Water Street. Atop an escarpment was the South Battery, and beyond it the King's Lime Kiln Yard Wharves. (The battery location now lies underneath Terminal Road and the Westin Hotel; the wharves' location is underneath the parking behind the Westin, extending towards present-day Pier 21 and Pier 22, which were built entirely on land fill). Straton's and Moorsom's later maps show the South Battery replaced by the huge, crescent-shaped Grand Battery, which remained in its location, now the intersection of Water Street and Terminal Road, until the 1880s.

Taken together, DesBarres's, Straton's, and Moorsom's maps show that before 1827 the waterfront to the south was less developed than the waterfront downtown, but it still had numerous buildings. The remains of some of these buildings now lie underneath the train yards and the residential complex east of the intersection of Barrington and Inglis streets. At this intersection, Freshwater Brook, having traversed much of the peninsula, entered the harbour.

What Maps Can Show Us

Opposite: J. F. DesBarres' map with a superimposed modern street grid and shoreline. This composite map, created by author Danny Dyke, shows that between 1878 and 2000 the Halifax street grid changed minimally, while the shoreline changed a great deal.

Maps, then, can show us a great deal. When georeferenced and digitized, they can show archaeologists precisely where development is likely to impact on hidden archaeological features. This eye-opening mapping technology has already been used to monitor development linked to the Halifax Harbour Solutions Project along Lower Water Street. The municipality of Halifax has sought to incorporate the technology into the management of its cultural resources by using it to identify more zones of high archaeological potential. As use of the technology expands, potential conflict between archaeologists and developers should be reduced; we can excavate and examine important sites first, and make way for the homes and businesses of Halifax's future.

Tales from the Crypt

Excavations Beneath the Little Dutch Church

Paul Williams, Queens University

N 1996, PLANNED REPAIRS TO THE FOUNDATIONS of the Little Dutch Church on Brunswick Street in Halifax's North End necessitated an archaeological investigation beneath the church. No excavation work of this kind had ever taken place in Halifax before. Indeed, while the archaeological excavation of church undercrofts is not

Left: Exterior of the Little Dutch Church, with the rector beside a tombstone in the cemetery..

Centre: The church during its use as a school, c.1870.

Right: Exterior of St. George's Round Church (with firefighting apparatus in foreground).

unusual in Europe—due to pressures of urban development, as well as conservation needs—it is rare in North America. Presenting both tremendous challenges and surprising results, work beneath the Little Dutch Church offered a fascinating glimpse of the burial history of early colonial Halifax.

Established in 1756 by German immigrants, the Little Dutch Church is a National Historic Site. It is the oldest Lutheran church in Canada, the first associated with German immigration, and one of only a few surviving eighteenth-century churches outside Quebec. Through the latter half of the eighteenth century it served the German community as a place of worship, community centre, and school. In the adjoining churchyard, the community buried its dead. By 1800, the congregation had outgrown its tiny building, and construction began on a new church (Saint George's Round Church) a block to the south. The spiritual role of the Little Dutch Church subsequently declined. However, in 1994, it returned to regular use after a fire badly damaged the Round Church. Renewed use highlighted the poor condition of the building and, in particular, its foundation walls. As a result, a restoration project was begun.

Crypt Clearance

Opposite: The Little Dutch Church, with the graveyard in the foreground.

Under the provincial *Special Places Protection Act*, the historical nature of the site required that the planned foundation repairs be preceded by an archaeological impact assessment. In the spring of 1996, the company In Situ, under the direction of Laird Niven and myself, was contracted to carry out the work beneath the church. The assessment was to include the investigation and clearance of three late-eighteenth-century

DUTCH TOWN It was not long after the founding of Halifax in 1749 that Governor Cornwallis declared his disappointment with the industry of many of his colonists. Writing to the British Board of Trade and Plantations, Cornwallis bemoaned the lack of industrious men willing to take an active role in carving the new settlement out of the wilderness. He reserved praise, however, for the small number of so-called foreign Protestants who had sailed with his expedition (perhaps seventy-nine of the 2,576 colonists were Continental European).

Taking the governor's words to heart, the Board of Trade and Plantations made the dramatic decision to recruit more foreign Protestants to colonize Nova Scotia. Between 1750 and 1752, roughly 2,500 foreign Protestants arrived in Halifax—nearly doubling the town's population. Of these new immigrants two-thirds were German. House lots for the German settlers were laid out in the North Suburbs, and the stretches of Brunswick, Gottingen, and Lockman streets marked with modest wooden cottages soon began to be known as Dutch (*Deutsche*) Town. –RP

brick crypts (so that the remains would not be jeopardized by the renovations), as well as test-pitting in the vicinity of the foundation walls.

On May 27, 1996, access to the undercroft of the church was gained through a hole cut in the floor beneath the steeple. What lay below was dark and cramped. In places, clearance was less than 0.3 metres, and it was never more than 1.0 metre. All around were piles of soil and rocks, thrown up during the crypt construction and by periods of later renovation. Above, the church was supported on a single-thickness, brick foundation wall, and the free-floating floor was propped by wooden pilings driven deep into

The undercroft of the Little Dutch Church clearly was a cramped place to conduct archaeological work. This view looks southward toward the crypts.

Damage to crypts, shown here, made it necessary for archaeologists to work very carefully.

the earth. Several of these canted under the weight of the joists. In other spots, the floor was borne on crossbeams lying in direct contact with the earth, making some areas of the undercroft completely inaccessible. It was clear that the logistics of excavating in such an environment would be extremely challenging.

At the southern end of the undercroft, the barrel vaults of two of the crypts were visible above the grade. Two adjoining crypts lay to the east and a single crypt to the west. Each had been heavily disturbed during previous work under the church, and debris and fallen bricks lay intermixed with human bones and coffin fragments. The primary task at hand was to remove and record all material from each crypt. While the clearance of the two adjoining crypts was relatively straightforward, the coffin in the western crypt was found to be partially undisturbed and required greater attention. The disarticulated remains were carefully removed and taken, along with those from the other crypts, to the physical anthropology laboratory at Saint Mary's University for safekeeping and analysis.

Who Was In the Crypts?

The crypts each contained the remains of a single individual. However, determining the identities of those buried there proved complicated. Conflicting historical information offered five different possibilities: Benjamin Gerrish (1709–1774), a New Englander who was storekeeper of the Royal Naval Dockyard and a member of the Colonial Council; the Reverend Bernard Michael Houseal (1727–1799), the first German-speaking minister of the Little Dutch Church; Major Leonard Lockman (c.1697–1769), a surgeon who arrived in Halifax with Governor Edward Cornwallis's expedition in 1749; Otto Wilhelm Schwartz (1715–1785), from the Prussian province of Livonia (now Latvia), who had also come with Cornwallis, as a fur trader; and Anna Justina Schwartz (c.1724–1784), wife of Otto.

Of these candidates, Gerrish is the least likely to have been buried at the Little Dutch Church. Despite the fact that he owned property in the vicinity, and Gerrish Street bears his name, there are no contemporary records to indicate that he was laid to rest at the church. On the other hand, a strong case may be made for Lockman, as his burial "in the German church" was recorded in the *Royal Gazette* on May 9, 1769. Moreover, his funerary hatchment hung in the church. Similarly, a plaque on the church's eastern wall records that Reverend B. M. Houseal was buried below the floor, a claim that is further supported by contemporary accounts. Meanwhile, other reports recall that Anna and Otto Schwartz were also buried in crypts beneath the church. The Schwartzes had been among the founders of Halifax (where they married in December 1750) and were promi-

THE GERMAN EVANGELICAL LUTHERAN CHURCH The size and status of the German community in Halifax in the 1750s is evident in the fact that Halifax's surveyor Charles Morris reserved a lot expressly for a German burial ground and church. In 1756, the community acquired a small barn which they transported to this lot at the northeast corner of Brunswick and Gerrish streets. Here it was set on new foundations and fitted with twelve rows of pews. It was the first Lutheran church in North America. –RP

Right: Nicole Lundrigan works carefully to uncover and then temporarily remove the remains for safekeeping.

nent members of the Little Dutch Church congregation until their deaths. Otto Schwartz was a church elder and a prime benefactor of the church's expansion and renovation in 1760. He accumulated a great deal of wealth, which was reflected in funeral costs.

The task of determining the identity of the crypt occupants fell to Nicole Lundrigan, a recent honours anthropology graduate of Saint Mary's University. While the contents of all three crypts had been heavily disturbed, Lundrigan was able to conclude that the occupants had all been elderly. In each case, there was evidence of ageing in the bones and joints, as well as heavy wear on the teeth, and thinning of the crania. Analysis also showed that the bones from the western crypt were those of a large man. Historical accounts suggest that Houseal fit such a profile, and a tentative identification was made on these grounds. Of the other two skeletons, Lundrigan concluded that one was a woman and the other a man. As only one woman, Anna Schwartz, is recorded as having been buried under the church, the remains of the former were identified as hers. It was further speculated that the bones from the adjoining crypt were most likely those of her husband, Otto. The Schwartzes had died within a year of each other, and all evidence points to the crypts having been built at the same time (sharing not only a common wall but also a common floor).

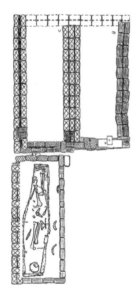

Above: A sketch of the crypts and contents. The two paired crypts, top, appear to have been constructed at the same time. The single crypt, bottom, shows outlines of a coffin with human remains.

A Mass Grave?

While the crypt clearance was underway, test pitting began in other areas of the church undercroft. Though limited by issues of accessibility, the testing was undertaken to verify an 1896 newspaper report, which had recorded the discovery of a number of skeletons in a shallow grave beneath the church during renovations. As there was no clear

Above: Author Paul Williams excavating a portion of the mass grave. The excavation proceeds cautiously in the vicinity of an exposed skull.

Below: The remains of two individuals buried around 1750 await temporary removal for safekeeping.

indication of where the bones had been encountered, nor where they were reburied, a number of areas were tested.

The 1996 testing quickly confirmed the accuracy of the 1896 report: in two test units, articulated human skeletons were encountered as little as 0.3 metres below the surface. By the time the archaeological impact assessment drew to a close, a minimum of ten skeletons had been exposed in what appeared to be a shallow trench. These individuals had been buried two deep and lying head to toe.

Extreme working conditions and the complex nature of the mass burial made progress slow. Coupled with financial constraints, this left the investigations unfinished in 1996. The bones of six individuals, however, were removed to Saint Mary's University for analysis, and the test pits were subsequently backfilled.

In 1998, following the construction of new concrete foundation walls, archaeological investigations continued beneath the Little Dutch Church. The intention of these inquiries was twofold: to complete the work begun in 1996, and to find suitable locations for the reburial of all the bones. The new foundations—along with the removal of old, derelict supports and beams—not only made the workspace much safer, but also allowed the entire undercroft to be better surveyed. In this new work environment, the 1756 northern foundation wall (the original north wall prior to the 1760 expansion of the church and addition of the steeple) was detectable, as was the 1896 reburial pit, which contained the partial remains of thirteen individuals (610 bones and bone fragments packed into a pit measuring approximately 0.8 metres in diameter and 0.5 metres deep). The remains from the reburial pit were excavated, as were those skeletons that had been left *in situ* (in their original location) in the original burial trench, uncovered in 1996. Their removal allowed the depth and nature of the burial area to be fully assessed.

From the beginning, it was clear that archaeologists were dealing with a mass grave. Mass graves were common in Europe from at least medieval times. Often associated with the poor, or victims of epidemic, a *fosse commune* (common trench) could measure as much as thirty metres long by five metres deep. Many hundred corpses were typically lowered into such pits, seldom in coffins, but sewn or tied into some sort of shroud or sacking, and layered unceremoniously, many deep and often head to toe, until the trench was filled.

On a smaller scale, the Little Dutch Church burials fit such a pattern. Indeed, rope samples were retrieved, suggesting at least one individual may have been tied into a sack. The burial trench itself varied in depth between 0.5 and 1.0 metre, and was capped with a layer of rocks. The church's western foundation wall delineated the western edge of the trench, while the eastern edge fell roughly along the median of the undercroft, making the mass grave approximately three metres wide. While its length could not be ascertained, its northernmost edge appeared to be at the original, pre-1760 foundation wall. This arrangement indicates that the church may have been purposefully erected above the grave, perhaps as an act of piety.

Identifying the Dead

The identification of the mass grave occupants proved to be a greater challenge than it was with those buried in the crypts. No historical evidence has survived documenting a mass burial on the site. The 1896 newspaper report suggests that the bones unearthed at that time were the remains of early German immigrants who had arrived in Halifax between 1750 and 1752. In making that assessment, inference was naturally drawn from their location beneath a church built by the German Lutheran community. The 1996 analysis followed suit. Likewise, the circumstances of death came to be inferred from accounts of widespread disease and subsequently high mortality rates in Halifax, following the arrival of German settlers aboard one of the immigrant ships, the *Ann*, in the autumn of 1750.

In 1998, anthropological analysis was carried out by Paul Erickson at Saint Mary's University. Using standard methods, he assessed the sex, age, stature, and overall health of each individual. Erickson concluded that the grave's occupants had been in generally good health prior to death and that they had been a relatively young population. (This contradicted the 1896 account which suggested that the German settlers had been elderly and sickly.) The cause of death, however, could not be determined. No pathological evidence was found for disease. Nevertheless, it was speculated that a virulent disease, such as ship's fever (or typhus), was the most plausible cause of death.

In his analysis, Erickson also entered bone measurements for fourteen specimens from the mass grave into FORDISC 2.0, a computerized forensic database. Based on comparison with modern forensic samples, FORDISC 2.0 generated statistical data for sex and race. In seven cases, the most probable racial grouping was declared to be black; in six, white; and in one, First Nations ("Native American"). While these results must be

EPIDEMIC ONBOARD THE *ANN* Before the hardship of life in the New World came the hardship of the ocean voyage. In the 1750s, the trans-Atlantic journey was fraught with disease. The eleven ships which carried the influx of so-called foreign Protestants to Halifax between 1750 and 1752 tended to be crowded and unsanitary. The drinking water was frequently contaminated. And while the recent innovation of shipboard ventilators was helping to reduce the risk of epidemic on the ocean crossing, the *Ann* was poorly ventilated.

When the *Ann* arrived in port at Halifax in September 1750, after twelve weeks at sea, seventeen of its 322 passengers were dead and many more were ill. (The disease is believed to have been typhus, which is spread by lice.) An epidemic subsequently broke out in the colony. By the time it could be contained, 333 Haligonians were dead, along with a large number of new immigrants who had made the crossing on the *Ann*. –RP

FORENSIC ANTHROPOLOGY AND FORDISC 2.0 Forensic anthropologists seek to attribute characteristics of the living—such as sex, age, ancestry, and stature—to unidentified bones of the dead. Examining and measuring bones, they compare their results to a database of bones that are already identified. In 1996, researchers at the Forensic Anthropology Center at the University of Tennessee, Knoxville, developed a computer program, FORDISC 2.0, to compare these measurements statistically. The program analyzes up to seventy-eight measurements of a skeleton to produce probability estimates—ranging from zero to one hundred percent—that the decedent was male or female and belonged to one or another of several ancestral groups (the chief ancestral groups are white, black, and American Indian).

The researchers developed FORDISC 2.0 to help anthropologists identify recent decedents, that is, people who died in the latter part of the twentieth century. For earlier decedents, therefore, the results of the analysis are less reliable. Consequently, when trying to identify eighteenth-century decedents—such as those buried beneath the Little Dutch Church—FORDISC 2.0 should be used cautiously and in conjunction with other identification techniques. –PE

interpreted with caution, the possibilities raised by this study warranted further investigation.

One specimen was singled out for further study: a partial cranium, labelled E66a, which had been retrieved from the 1896 reburial pit. The cranium exhibited slightly shovelled incisors, severe tooth wear, and broad facial features. Although these characteristics are often more commonly associated with First Nations rather than European peoples, no definitive statement of ancestry could be made from a visual inspection. From his analyses, Erickson simply concluded that E66a was the only specimen that could not be excluded as First Nations. Although the analytic methods were unable to provide clear-cut answers, additional evidence supported the hypothesis that E66a was not European. Attention was drawn to the degree and flat nature of the wear on the teeth. Such wear, in a young adult, is more consistent with someone of First Nations origin; it is characteristic of someone whose diet contains many gritty foods—roots, nuts, seeds, and meat.

The discovery of E66a challenged the previous assumption that all of those buried in the mass grave were Europeans. Historical association and the physical context had pointed clearly to the latter interpretation. So who, then, was E66a? Was he Mi'kmaq? Was he Protestant or Catholic? How did he come to be buried in the mass grave?

His burial in a Protestant cemetery outside an eighteenth-century English settlement would seem to indicate that he was not Mi'kmaq. At the time, the Mi'kmaq were not only allied with the French but had also largely converted to Roman Catholicism. Regrettably, there is little documentary evidence of a First Nations presence in mid-eighteenth-century Halifax. The notable exceptions were John Goreham's Rangers, Mohawks of mixed ancestry who had been brought to the new colony in 1749 to counter Mi'kmaw raids. There is also a lone reference to the burial of one John Tray, "Protestant Indian," in the Saint Paul's burial register for August 27, 1750.

Beyond the possible First Nations representation in the burial sample, we might also consider the potential African presence. Prior to black Loyalist immigration, there were perhaps as many as five hundred African slaves in Nova Scotia. Most were domestic servants of British or New England colonists, although some were involved in the construction of Halifax. The *Boston Evening Post* of September 1751, for example, announced that, "Just arrived from Halifax and to be sold, ten strong, hearty Negro men, mostly tradesmen...." There were also "free Blacks" in Halifax in the 1750s.

The possible African connections with the site remain, at present, vague. Certainly, it is likely that wealthier members of the German community had African servants. Recorded on the passenger manifest for the Cornwallis expedition in 1749, for example, were seven servants of Leonard Lockman. That Lockman had, at the very least, a tacit connection with slavery is evident in a newspaper advertisement in the *Halifax Gazette* on May 15, 1752, which announced: "Just imported, and to be sold by Joshua Mauger, at Major Lockman's store in Halifax, several Negro slaves."

Reburial

Despite the historical inferences, no firm answers have yet been found as to the identity of the skeletons from the mass grave. Indeed, it is unclear whether historical identities may ever be established. Nevertheless, excavation beneath the Little Dutch Church presented the exceptional opportunity to study not only two different periods of burial but two very different burial practices in the same historic site. The identification of the occupants of the crypts and the anthropological study of the remains from the mass grave offered new insight into the early history of the church and of Halifax itself.

From the beginning, it had been agreed that all remains would be reburied at the end of the project. On August 25, 1998, all the bones were re-interred beneath the church, following a service of recommital and a Mi'kmaw sweetgrass ceremony.

The archaeological investigations were carried out by In Situ under the direction of Laird Niven and myself. The project benefitted from the help of a number of individuals: Danny Dyke, Paul Erickson, Kent Hodges, Brent Hueber, Nicole Lundrigan, Michael MacMaster, and April Mitchell. Additional assistance was provided by Don Cunningham and Bruce Wright of the Faculty of Dentistry at Dalhousie University; Gwyneth Jones of the Department of Biology at Saint Mary's University; and Stephen Davis of the Department of Anthropology at Saint Mary's University.

Location, Location, Location!

Archaeological Mitigation on the Halifax Wastewater Treatment Property

W. Bruce Stewart, Cultural Resource Management Group Limited

THROUGHOUT THE 1990s the state of Halifax Harbour was increasingly a cause of public concern. It was generally agreed that the longstanding practise of pumping untreated sewage into the harbour was unsustainable. However, the question of how to address this problem had no simple solutions. Towards the end of the decade—following a series of task forces, committees, and public hearings—the Halifax Regional Municipality (HRM) made a commitment to build three advanced, primary-level wastewater treatment plants (WTPs), in Halifax, Dartmouth, and Herring Cove. The first of these facilities was to be constructed on a municipally owned property located at Barrington and Cornwallis streets on the Halifax waterfront.

The historical significance of the property was formally identified during the course of an environmental site assessment undertaken in 1999. As part of a multi-disciplinary study team, Cultural Resource Management (CRM) Group conducted an archaeological screening study that reviewed historic land use within the proposed development property to identify areas of archaeological potential. The review provided much documentary evidence indicating the property had been intensively occupied since the founding of Halifax in 1749. Despite the cycle of demolition and redevelopment that extended into the latter half of the twentieth century, it was recommended that the proposed WTP site undergo a full archaeological impact assessment. In July 2002, CRM Group was again retained by HRM to undertake the recommended assessment. The assessment, designed to test areas of archaeological potential identified in the screening report, yielded a wide range of structural remains and artifacts reflecting late-eighteenth- to late-twentieth-century life within the property.

In October 2002, CRM Group was retained once more to conduct archaeological mitigation within the proposed Halifax WTP site. The objective was to identify, document, and interpret significant archaeological resources within specific areas of the property, and thus mitigate the impact of redevelopment. Based on the results of the impact assessment and recommendations from the Nova Scotia Museum (which regulates archaeological work in the province), excavation was focussed on the northern half of the block, bounded by a tree line. Archaeological fieldwork was conducted between November 4 and December 5, 2002, by a twenty-member team of archaeologists. Post-fieldwork analysis, interpretation, and documentation incorporated material culture analysts, historians, and conservators into the core archaeology team.

Site History

Previous page: Manual excavation in the northwest corner of the WTP site is well underway, while mechanical stripping continues to the south.

British Halifax was founded in 1749 with the survey of the town site and establishment of the Royal Naval Dockyard to the north ten years later. In conjunction with the survey of the town, the north and south suburbs were also delineated (outside of the town fortifications). Due to its position relative to the town and the dockyard, the north suburbs developed first. Brunswick Street and Upper Water Street (which hugged the shoreline) were

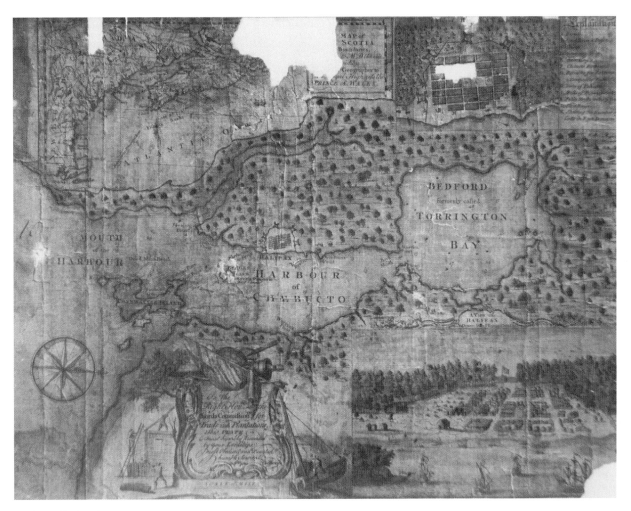

Halifax and harbour in 1750. The WTP property is located in the area of Bing's Beach, midway between the 1749 town site and Gorham's (Goreham's) Point, site of the Royal Naval Dockyard.

the primary north–south arteries between the town and the dockyard, and Cornwallis Street and Proctor's Lane were important east–west connectors.

Situated within the north suburbs, what is now the WTP property occupied a steeply sloped stretch of shoreline midway between the town and the Royal Naval Dockyard. The property wrapped around a broad cove that was bisected by a small stream flowing east from the area of the North Common. The 1749 survey divided the WTP property west of Upper Water Street into seven lots (A12 through A18). Lot A12, bordering on the south side of Cornwallis Street, was 50 feet (15.2 metres) wide, while the remaining lots were a full 100 feet (30.4 metres) wide. The depths of the lots ranged from a maximum of 260 feet (79.2 metres) to a minimum of 210 feet (64.0 metres). The difference in lot depth reflected the irregularities of the shoreline. Between 1749 and 1753 all of this land was granted to colonists, and by 1759, a house had been built on each of the seven lots.

The water lots located opposite the study area, on the east side of Upper Water Street, were also granted in the early years of the settlement. In less than a decade, maps began to show a number of named wharves along this stretch of the Halifax shoreline. Bernard's Dock, Ives Wharf, and Proctor's Wharf bear the names of several of the earliest entrepreneurs to develop commercial interests on these water lots. Based on the old adage, "location is everything," the WTP site's position on the waterfront between the town site and the dockyard established the property as an important piece of eighteenth-century real estate.

However, the rapid infilling of the shoreline with wharves, interspersed with warehouses, shops, and boarding houses, was not matched by the same level of development on the adjacent WTP property. Although buildings had been erected on each of the lots, the lack of rear access slowed the infilling of the block. It would not be until the 1870s—with the extension of Lockman Street south of Cornwallis—that development extended beyond the street fronts of Upper Water and Cornwallis streets.

In the last quarter of the nineteenth century, the character of the WTP property changed dramatically. Construction of the Nova Scotia Railway in the 1850s, with its Duffus Street terminal, and later the North Street terminal of the Intercolonial Railway, created traffic congestion along Upper Water Street. To provide an additional north–south artery, Barrington Street was pushed north to connect with Lockman, diverting through traffic away from the busy commercial activities concentrated along Upper Water Street. The new Barrington Street also prompted development of the western portions of Lots A12 through A18, which had been largely inaccessible. Furthermore, the opening of the Intercolonial Railway's Deep Water Terminal in the area around 1880 prompted modernization and expansion of wharves and commercial buildings along Upper Water Street to the north of the study site, between Gerrish and Cornwallis streets.

Based on the old adage, "location is everything," the WTP site's position on the waterfront established the property as an important piece of eighteenth-century real estate.

Based on the detailed information published in city directories and fire insurance plans introduced in the 1870s, the WTP property at the time can be characterized as a balance of residential and commercial occupation. Area residents were primarily working class: a mix of carpenters, roofers, labourers, shoemakers, tailors, coopers, carters, and tinsmiths, as well as ship builders and mariners. Commercial interests included a range of shops—typically grocery, variety, and liquor stores—as well as hotels and boarding houses.

Southward expansion of the rail lines soon prompted the introduction of light industrial and manufacturing elements into the residential and commercial mix. Cunard's Coal Yard had long dominated the southern portion of the WTP property. By the 1870s, J. J. Scriven and Son's Bakery occupied a warren of buildings extending from Upper Water Street through to Barrington. Felix J. Quinn established a bottling plant in a building at the rear of the European Hotel in the late 1860s before moving from this Upper Water Street location to an expanded facility on the newly opened Barrington

Street. Other interests operating in the study area during this period included W. W. Howell & Company, a firm of brass founders, mechanical engineers, and machinists, and Mahar's Transfer Express.

The late-nineteenth-century mix of residential, commercial, and light industrial development within the WTP property is reflected in a photograph taken from the top of the adjacent grain elevator in 1902. Examples of Scottish-Georgian style attached houses were evident extending south and west from the corner of Upper Water and Cornwallis streets, as well as along Cornwallis Lane, a narrow lane running south from Cornwallis Street into the centre of the property. The remainder of the property, meanwhile, is clearly dominated by the newer, late-Victorian style row houses and flat-roofed commercial buildings.

This view across the WTP property, c.1902, from the adjacent grain elevator reveals a late nineteenth-century urban mix of residential, commercial, and light industrial development.

During the first half of the twentieth century, the WTP property entered a prolonged period of economic decline. The occupants and ownership of the various buildings changed on a fairly regular basis. Despite the brief economic booms related to World Wars One and Two, residential and commercial activities within the property continued to suffer. Businesses failed and residents departed, leaving many buildings vacant. The inter-war introduction of two new heavy commercial interests—a plumbing and heating firm, and a manufacturer of mirrors and other glass products—further changed the character of the property.

Plans for post-war urban renewal ultimately brought about the demise of residential occupation within the study area. Although various commercial enterprises survived until the year 2000, the early Scottish-Georgian row houses were gone by 1950, and by 1980 what is now the WTP property was largely abandoned.

Excavation of the WTP site

Archaeological mitigation within the WTP property began on November 4, 2002, with the mechanical stripping of the study area. An excavator fitted with a toothless bucket was used to strip recent fill and overburden from an area of approximately thirty-two hundred square metres. This footprint corresponded to at least half a dozen nineteenth-century lots, with their associated residential, commercial, and ancillary structures. All mechanical excavation was carefully monitored by members of the archaeological field

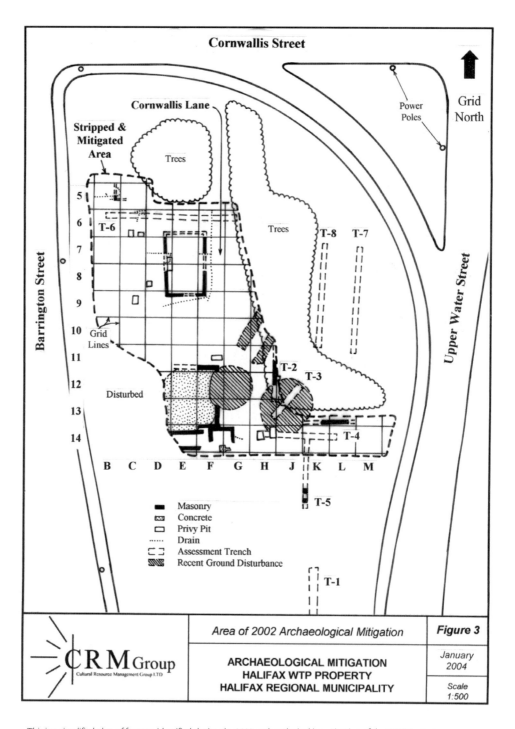

Cornwallis Street

Cornwallis Lane

Grid
North

Power
Poles

**Stripped &
Mitigated
Area**

Trees

5

6   T-6

7

8

9

10   Grid
Lines

11

12   Disturbed

13

14

B   C   D   E   F   G   H   J   K   L   M

Trees

Trees   T-8   T-7

T-2   T-3

T-4

T-5

Barrington Street

Upper Water Street

■   Masonry
⊠   Concrete
▭   Privy Pit
······   Drain
⊏ ⊐   Assessment Trench
▨   Recent Ground Disturbance

T-1

CRM Group	Area of 2002 Archaeological Mitigation	**Figure 3**
Cultural Resource Management Group LTD	**ARCHAEOLOGICAL MITIGATION HALIFAX WTP PROPERTY HALIFAX REGIONAL MUNICIPALITY**	January 2004
		Scale 1:500

This is a simplified plan of features identified during the 2002 archaeological investigation of the WTP property.

crew to minimize impact on the underlying resources. When potentially significant archaeological features were encountered by the excavator, work was suspended until closer inspection was made. If the find was considered to be significant, the excavator was directed to work in another area of the site, so that the resource could be properly studied and documented.

Early in the mechanical excavation, a master grid was established on the site to provide horizontal control over all architectural features and artifacts uncovered. As the sub-grade surface expanded, patterns started to emerge that defined properties, yards, areas of activity, and outbuildings. Manual excavation techniques were used to uncover the boundaries of these landscape features and prepare for documentation and testing, or full excavation.

During the course of the field program, the combination of mechanical and manual excavation techniques exposed approximately fifteen major features—consisting of seven structures (residential or commercial buildings) and eight privies—as well as a complex web of stone, wood, and ceramic drains. The most substantial structural remains included the following: the early-nineteenth-century Scottish-Georgian style row house located along the east side of Cornwallis Lane; the Victorian-style row houses built along Barrington Street, circa 1875; the Saint Patrick's Young Men's Temperance Hall built on Barrington in 1890; and turn-of-the-century commercial/industrial buildings erected to accommodate the western expansion of both J. J. Scriven and Son's Bakery and the newly established W. W. Howell & Company, a general machine shop. Given the relatively late construction dates for most of these structures, however, and their occupation well into the twentieth century, it is more significant to consider the features found in the yards adjoining these structures—many of which survived the late-nineteenth-century subdivision and redevelopment of the WTP property. Among these features was a diverse selection of privies and drains.

Top left: Initial stages of site stripping. Mechanical excavators were used to remove modern overburden from the WTP site prior to manual cleanup and excavation.

Top right: Manual excavation underway. Manual excavation quickly followed the mechanical stripping of modern overburden. Excavation within the northwest corner of the WTP site revealed the ironstone slabs used to support the floor joists in the basement of this house, which faced onto Barrington Street.

Bottom left: These privy vaults represent two of the eight privies identified during archaeological mitigation of the WTP property.

Investigating another soil stain. Examination of the stripped surface of the site revealed a number of stains or discolourations in the soil. Manual excavatioin of this particular stain revealed one of the wood-lined privies found at various locations across the WTP site.

Privies, Drains, and Refuse

It is somewhat ironic that privies are the most common feature at the site of a future wastewater treatment facility. The eight identified privies reflect a range of abandonment dates, from the 1840s through the early twentieth century. The privies had all been wood-lined but ranged significantly in size. The smallest of the privies, abandoned around 1900, measured 1.15 metres by 0.90 metres, while the largest, also abandoned in the early twentieth century, measured 1.70 metres by 2.60 metres. A comparison of dimensions suggests that the privies represent a mix of one- and two-person facilities.

As expected, the privies were a convenient receptacle for the disposal of domestic refuse, particularly at the time of a building's abandonment. As a consequence, the eight privies together accounted for approximately seventy-two percent of the more than 26,800 artifacts recovered from the WTP property. Actual artifact counts ranged from a low of 1,285 artifacts recovered from the smallest privy (abandoned around 1900) to a high count of 4,610 artifacts recovered from one of

Far right: Nineteenth-century spoons. Two copper alloy spoons (one gold plate) recovered from Privy 8.

the two privies abandoned in the 1850s. The count averaged approximately 2,400 artifacts per privy. While the collections of artifacts recovered from the eight privies contained a range of domestic items, the vast majority (between 86.5 percent and 99 percent) were ceramics and glass. In all but one of the privies, ceramics outnumbered glass artifacts by a significant margin. Other artifact types recovered from the privies included clay smoking pipes, buttons (metal, glass, and bone), straight pins, thimbles, thread spools, marbles, coins, lead bullets, leather shoes, wooden scrub brushes, tooth brushes, nails, tool handles, tools, and waste food bones. Individual items of particular interest included a door knob, a walking stick, and a cannonball.

Taken in the context of the detailed property histories compiled for the site, the recovered artifacts provided valuable insight into the social and economic realities of the former residents of the WTP property.

More notable features found on the study site were the networks of stone, wood, and ceramic drains that laced across

Transfer print plate. Brown transfer print on refined white earthenware plate recovered from Privy 7.

the property. The drainage system comprised various elements that reflected the evolution of drains and sewage collection in the urban setting. The earliest elements consisted of wooden box drains and simple ironstone spillways with wooden bases. As these early elements silted up or rotted away, the system was upgraded by introducing ceramic and then cast-iron piping. As later systems often followed the same alignment as the original wood or rock drains, remains of the earlier elements were often fragmentary. Elements of the drainage system were exposed. They ran below, through, and around buildings, indicating the age of the drain relative to the adjacent building.

Other Finds

Far right: Stoneware chamber pot recovered from Privy 1.

Below: Blue shell edge pearlware plate recovered from Privy 7.

In addition to the privies and drains, the month-long excavation yielded a small number of other significant discoveries that contributed to the overall interpretation of the WTP property. Careful examination of the ground surface within the alignment of Cornwallis Lane revealed an east–west oriented series of post moulds. Some quick calculations confirmed that the post moulds were the remnants of a fence line that once marked the boundary between Lots A13 and A14. It also proved to define the eastern side of Cornwallis Lane. Further examination of the ground surface in the area of the fence line identified a distinct layer of light brown sandy silt extending south from the fence line to the western and southern limits of the unit. The layer was sandwiched between an overlying fill deposit and the underlying sterile subsoil. Excavation of this thin soil deposit yielded a wide range of late-eighteenth- to mid-nineteenth-century domestic arti-

HARBOUR PROBLEMS DEMAND HARBOUR SOLUTIONS Halifax Harbour is one of the world's best deepwater, ice-free ports. However, 250 years of polluting the harbour have taken their toll on this great resource. Every day more than 181,000,000 litres of untreated sanitary and storm wastewater empty into Halifax Harbour. As a result, bacterial contamination is widespread, with the presence of floatables marring the beauty of the Halifax and Dartmouth waterfronts.

The issues of sewage treatment and harbour cleanup have been debated by municipal politicians for decades. And while treatment facilities were built at Mill Cove and Eastern Passage in the early 1970s, the majority of sewage continues to empty into the harbour untreated. In 1997, the newly minted Halifax Regional Municipality inaugurated the Halifax Harbour Solutions Project, with the goal of eliminating the flow of raw sewage and other contaminants into the harbour. The succession of studies, recommendations, assessments, and bids that followed bore tangible results on June 15, 2004, when Mayor Peter Kelly signed the $133 million contract with D&D Water Solutions for the construction of three wastewater treatment plants, in Halifax, Dartmouth, and Herring Cove, to open in 2006, 2007, and 2008 respectively. –RP

Cleanup along Cornwallis Lane. Removal of the loose material left behind by the excavator revealed various trenches and features in this area of Cornwallis Lane.

facts. While representing only about 2 percent of the total site assemblage, the 568 artifacts recovered came from the earliest occupation layer yet identified on the WTP property. This sheet midden was a collection of domestic refuse—including a wide range of ceramics (earthenware, stoneware, creamware, pearlware, and porcelain), both window and bottle glass, and pipe stems and bowls—that survived simply by chance. After the refuse was strewn here, subsequent cycles of development continued to add fill to the landscape, keeping these artifacts undisturbed in their original context by burying them. Discoveries such as this highlight the importance of looking beyond hard architectural features, like masonry walls, privies, and drains, to the less tangible but equally important stains and colour changes in the soil.

Further Consideration

Although formal excavation on the WTP property concluded in early December 2002, there were still areas of the property that warranted further archaeological consideration. In the fall of 2004, CRM Group archaeologists were back on the site to monitor all construction-related excavation undertaken by the developer. Monitoring was required due to lingering concerns that remnants of structures from the late eighteenth and early nineteenth centuries could still lie buried beneath more recent foundations.

Focusing on the southern half of the WTP property, excavators stripped fill and topsoil to expose the remains of late-nineteenth- and twentieth-century commercial and residential buildings fronting on Upper Water and Barrington streets. All work was conducted under the watchful eyes of experienced urban archaeologists. Through the cooperation of the supervisory staff and equipment operators, it was possible to investigate and document the masonry features before they were demolished and the rubble removed from the site.

Piece by piece, the features and artifacts found in the excavation of the Wastewater Treatment Plant property filled in the history of this waterfront lot in the old north suburbs, offering an important document of 250 years of urban development.

A Walk in the Park

Point Pleasant Park
after Hurricane Juan

Lynne Schwarz
Fred Schwarz
Black Spruce Heritage Services

I N THE EARLY MORNING HOURS of Monday, September 29, 2003, Halifax was hit by Hurricane Juan. With winds of up to 182 kilometres per hour, it was the worst hurricane to strike the city since 1893. The next morning, Halifax's streets were a tangle of downed trees and power lines. Two deaths were attributed to the storm, and property damage was widespread. A state of emergency was declared, and Canadian Armed Forces troops were called in to assist in the cleanup. Some three hundred thousand homes were left without electricity; in many neighbourhoods, it was well over a week before power was restored.

Point Pleasant Park after Hurricane Juan.

Some of the most telling images of the damage caused by Hurricane Juan came from Point Pleasant Park, a seventy-five-hectare, heavily wooded urban park located at the southern tip of the Halifax peninsula. Prior to Hurricane Juan, the park was best known for its walking trails, lined with majestic pines, spruce, and birch, leading to shoreline views of Halifax Harbour and the Northwest Arm. Amongst the trees, glades contained the remains of well-known military fortifications dating from the eighteenth, nineteenth, and twentieth centuries. After Hurricane Juan, some fifty-seven thousand trees—seventy percent of all the trees in Point Pleasant Park—had either been uprooted, broken, or snagged. There are many speculations about the reasons for the heavy damage, but the track of the storm, the "over-mature" woodland, and the scarce topsoil cover in the park were likely contributing factors. Though the tree falls damaged some historic structures in the park, it is an ill wind that blows no good: the uprooted landscape created by the hurricane also offered a unique opportunity for archaeologists to see what lay underground.

Although much of Halifax Regional Municipality had suffered damage in the storm, the severe impact on Point Pleasant Park very quickly became a focus of attention. Clean-up and remediation of the damage began in January 2004, with forestry companies, professional foresters, and archaeologists continuing work through the winter and spring. The archaeological concern was to minimize unintended impacts of heavy forestry equipment upon historic remains. Monitoring the removal of downed trees from

Previous page: This recent photograph shows roughly the same view as that painted by Colonel A. C. Mercer in 1842 (see p.80).

the major fortifications was perhaps the easiest task. More difficult was identifying out-lying military features and the even subtler remains of early settlement so they could be marked and avoided by the heavy logging equipment. Most of these features had never been surveyed and were now invisible beneath a blanket of downed trees and snow. As part of the archaeological work, all the exposed root masses of toppled and leaning trees were surveyed. Peering under the skirts of these fallen *grande dames* was a daunting task, but it proved to be extremely rewarding: about 150 tree root masses revealed arti-facts dating to the early settlement or military use of the park.

The History of Point Pleasant Park

Point Pleasant's pre-contact (pre-European) history is little known, although those of us who conducted the archaeology did find a tantalizing trace. It is known that Mi'kmaw attacks on early settlers were still a problem in the Point Pleasant area until 1759.

FOR A SHILLING Since 1866, Point Pleasant Park has been leased to the people of Halifax by the British Crown at the cost of one shilling per year. Each summer a ceremony takes place at the Prince of Wales Tower for the Halifax Regional Municipality to render payment to the Lieutenant Governor (or other representative of the Queen). Following the ceremony, the shilling is generously returned to the HRM for use the following year. The lease will expire in 2865. –RP

Initially selected by Governor Cornwallis as the site for the new town of Halifax in 1749, Point Pleasant was instead laid out as farming and fishing lots outside the city. By 1752, most of what is now the park had been granted to settlers to be cleared, farmed, and settled. Over time, this land was increasingly consolidated into larger and larger parcels by some of the area's most prominent land owners, including Joseph Gerrish and Lieutenant-Governor Edmund Fanning. Though some of the early farm roads survive today as park trails, there is now little visible evidence of this early settlement. Subsequently, one of the most challenging archaeological tasks of the post-hurricane cleanup was to locate, record, and protect features from this period.

The conspicuous military fortifications, meanwhile, are a constant reminder of a different chapter of the park's history—testifying to Point Pleasant's service in guarding the approaches to Halifax since its founding. What are now the Point Pleasant and Northwest Arm Batteries were first built in 1762; Chain Battery and a large entrenchment was added in 1778; Fort Ogilvie was built in 1793; and the Prince of Wales Tower was constructed from 1796 to 1798. With changes in military technology, these defences were periodically upgraded (such as Fort Ogilvie in the 1860s and again in 1899), and new fortifications added (for instance, Cambridge Battery in the 1860s). However, due to changing military and political contexts, by 1900 the Point Pleasant defences were largely redundant, though Fort Ogilvie remained armed as late as World War Two.

From the outset a popular destination for strolls and picnics, Point Pleasant was formally established as a park in 1873, just as its military role was about to decline. Hundreds of trees were planted, early roadways were converted to walking paths, and new trails were cut. Before the turn of the century, new structures were erected, including two summer houses (1800s) and the Superintendent's Lodge (1896-1897).

Map of Point Pleasant Park. The numbered stars identify the stops mentioned in the text. Stop 1 is the Lodge Entrance; Stop 2, the Prince of Wales Tower; Stop 3, Cambridge Battery; Stop 4, Northwest Arm Battery; Stop 5, Point Pleasant Battery; Stop 6, Prince of Wales Drive and Heather Road; and Stop 7, Green Field.

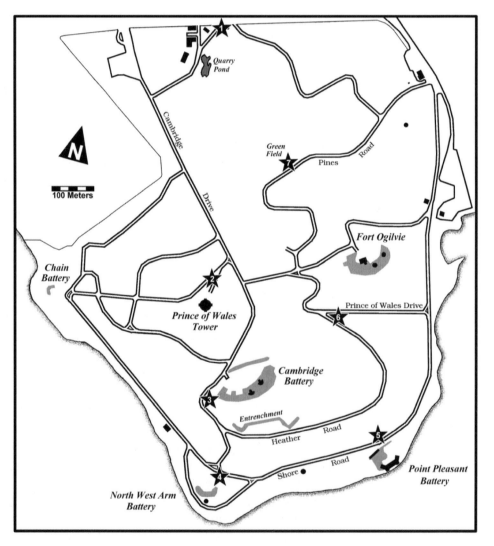

A Walking Tour of Point Pleasant's Archaeology

Many people may not be aware that the closed-canopy forest shading the paths of Point Pleasant before Hurricane Juan hit on September 29, 2003, was not a primary forest, nor even a very old one. The original forest was cleared from most of the park soon after 1750 for timber, and to create fields and pasture. Probably by 1800, white spruce and other trees began to reclaim some of the old fields, though the sight lines for the major fortifications were kept relatively clear through most of the nineteenth century. Many historic photographs and paintings from most of the historic period depict Point Pleasant as a more open, "domesticated" landscape than it is today. Even the forest that became established in the last 100 to 150 years was very much a product of human intervention.

Above all, Point Pleasant Park is a place for strolling. The best way to see the park as it is today, and to imagine it as it was in the past, is to walk its paths and make some stops along the way. Such a stroll might well begin at the gates by the Superintendent's Lodge.

The Lodge Entrance

From the entrance near the Superintendent's Lodge, a path leads into the park past Quarry Pond. The only permanent body of water in the park, this pond has formed in the quarry that was probably a source of stone for the Prince of Wales Tower, built at the end of the eighteenth century. A little farther down the path, the archaeological survey team discovered small sherds of creamware, found in tree throws. This ceramic ware, common from the 1770s to the 1820s, may date to the time the quarry was in use, although it would be surprising to find fine tableware at a quarry site. An archived mortgage document, however, does refer to a house in this area as early as 1753. It is not known how long this house stood, nor precisely where it stood, but the creamware sherds hint that it may have been somewhere nearby.

The Prince of Wales Tower

The Prince of Wales Tower, shown around 1870.

Turning onto Cambridge Drive, the stroller now follows one of the earliest roadways in the park, which dates to the 1780s (if not earlier), and comes at length to the Prince of Wales Tower. This fortification was built by Prince Edward, the Duke of Kent (father of Queen Victoria), while he was stationed in Halifax as commander of the British troops in Nova Scotia; an amateur architect, the prince took a keen interest in the improvement of Halifax's defences. The Prince of Wales Tower once offered commanding views across the Northwest Arm and the Halifax Harbour, and now, after the devastation of the hurricane, it does so once more. Perhaps the best-known structure in the park, designated a National Historic Site, the tower stands complete and intact, although modified somewhat from its original 1798 design. Originally, the tower had mounted cannon to defend the Northwest Arm and to protect the shore batteries against attack from the rear, but, in the 1860s, it was converted into a self-defending magazine. Additionally, the foundation of a small guardhouse still remains in the woods nearby, although it is not clearly visible from the road. Even less conspicuous is the refuse left behind by the tower's garrison: bottle glass, ceramics, and other artifacts dating from the early- to middle-nineteenth century, which had been concealed by soil and underbrush for 150 years, but identified during remediation work. One surprising find among this debris was a small polished stone axe-head, likely dating back to the Ceramic (or Maritime Woodland) Period, between 2,500 and 500 years ago. This tool was the first and only evidence for a pre-(European) contact Mi'kmaw presence at Point Pleasant.

Cambridge Battery

To the southeast of the Prince of Wales Tower lie the remains of Cambridge Battery, the last major fortification to be built at Point Pleasant. Though remodeled in the 1870s, much of the brick structure was built in the 1860s. Most visitors to the park are familiar with the central "courtyard" of the battery, often used as a venue for the open-air

Cambridge Battery, built 1862–68, was named after the Duke of Cambridge, commander-in-chief of the British army for more than four decades.

Shakespeare by the Sea theatre. Even after the hurricane, the courtyard remains a leafy glade. On initial assessment, tree falls over the brick and concrete structures of the battery looked alarming but proved relatively easy to remove; however, tree falls in the defensive ditch south of the main battery were extensive and caused some damage to the earthworks. In its military heyday, Cambridge Battery was surrounded by many auxiliary structures, including a powder magazine and laboratory, barracks, and canteen, the remains of which had to be identified and protected during remediation. A popular attraction just south of the battery is the unusual patch of Scottish heather, thought to have been introduced accidentally (perhaps as stuffing in bedrolls) when the area was used as a military campsite in the 1850s. Careful inspection will reveal that the heather patches have spread over a subtle ridge, the faint remains of a 171-metre-long entrenchment excavated as a defensive earthwork during the American War of Independence in 1778. This earthwork is clearly visible on Charles Blaskowitz's 1784 map of Halifax. Its precise defensive function remains unclear.

Hurricane damage in Cambridge Battery. Some tree falls on the battery were relatively easy to remove, while others, in the defensive ditch south of the battery, caused damage to the earthworks.

Downslope and just across Heather Road from the entrenchment sits another, smaller earthwork. This small field battery was thrown up in 1855 as a military exercise and never formed part of the point's defenses. Walker Battery, as it is known, was so densely covered by fallen trees that it was invisible at the start of remediation work. Two large pine trees removed during the work appeared to be approximately 150 years old and must have become established almost immediately after the earthwork was constructed.

Northwest Arm Battery

On a drumlin behind the shoreline in the southwest corner of the park stands Northwest Arm Battery. Constructed somewhat hastily in 1762, then rebuilt in 1778 and again around 1812, its guns were intended to defend the Arm, but it became obsolete relatively quickly. Thus, it still retains its early nineteenth-century configuration. This battery had become densely forested, rendering it almost fully obscured by trees when the storm struck. After the hurricane, large tree trunks straddled the earthworks, and removing them without damage to the structure proved complicated. Fortunately, the summer house in front of the battery (erected in 1886) survived a tree fall on its roof with little damage. Now the battery is clearly visible, and stands as probably the most substantial early earthwork surviving in the park. The massive tree throws in this area not only revealed artifacts discarded by the fort's garrison in the late-eighteenth and early-nineteenth centuries (such as bottle glass, ceramics, and clay pipe fragments), but also yielded important clues to the approximate location of the garrison barracks as well.

Point Pleasant Battery

Like Northwest Arm Battery, Point Pleasant Battery was constructed in 1762, then upgraded once in 1778 and again circa 1812. It too became obsolete by the middle of the nineteenth century, but between the 1880s and World War One, it was re-armed and equipped with searchlights and a powerhouse to support the submarine minefield defending the harbour. Today, it is these later-built, concrete facilities that are visible, while the original earthwork can no longer be recognized. The fortifications suffered no damage from fallen trees; however, the many downed trees lying across nearby Shore Road revealed an extraordinary amount of artifacts from the late eighteenth and early nineteenth centuries. The sheer volume of artifacts discovered, such as bottle glass, ceramics, clay pipe fragments, windowpane glass, and brick fragments, as well as pieces of both burnt and unburnt animal bone, suggests that this concentration of debris was deposited after the demolition of a barracks. Like the artifact deposits near Northwest Arm Battery and the Prince of Wales Tower, there is a remarkable amount of hidden information here, which could reveal much about daily life in the outlying garrisons of Halifax between the 1770s and the 1870s.

An 1842 watercolour sketch by Colonel A. C. Mercer. The sketch looks south from what is now Heather Road toward Point Pleasant Battery.

A small cliff rises north of the battery and, on higher ground, remediation work revealed possible foundation remains, as well as several concentrations of artifacts (creamware, pearlware, porcelain, glass) dating from 1770 to 1830. This was something of a surprise, as no barracks are known to have stood on the site, and there are no definite references to civilian houses, either. An 1842 watercolour by Colonel A. C. Mercer of the Royal Engineers, entitled "Point Pleasant Battery etc…from my fields," shows an old fieldstone wall north of Point Pleasant Battery, but clearly no buildings were standing by that date. Interestingly, the title of the sketch implies that Mercer's own quarters may have been somewhere nearby, presumably behind the painter's view. It is also interesting that, even after the devastation of Hurricane Juan, the view across Point Pleasant Battery is more wooded now than it was in August of 1842, when Mercer sat down to paint.

Prince of Wales Drive and Heather Road

Where Prince of Wales Drive (another of the early roads) joins with Heather Road, a small grassy glade with two picnic tables makes a convenient stop. To the north rises the escarpment of Fort Ogilvie. After Hurricane Juan, this high, steep escarpment was a considerable challenge to clear of fallen trees, with foresters and archaeologists monitoring to ensure that the frozen slopes were not damaged by the harvesting machines. Nothing of the original 1793 battery remains on site, and everything to be seen at Fort Ogilvie today dates to the 1860s or later. Looking south, the slopes down toward the harbour were once open fields enclosed by stone walls, as shown in Blaskowitz's map of 1784, and sections of these old field walls still survive today. With historic maps in hand, and working closely with remediation crews, the archaeologists were able to locate most of these sections of wall, despite the snow cover, to prevent them from being crushed under the wheels of the logging machines. Several tree throws in this area yielded eighteenth-century artifacts, and it seems likely that Lieutenant Governor

Fanning's house, sold by him to the military in 1793 (along with the land for Fort Ogilvie), once stood somewhere nearby.

Green Field

Continuing along Pine Road, the final stop on our itinerary is the picnic glade called Green Field. Remediation work first began not far from here, with logging supervisors and consultants scrambling across the frozen slopes on a sunny January day to select a test area for the remediation process. For the archaeologists, this is where the project

Artillery practice at Fort Ogilvie, c.1904.

ended as well. Blakowitz's map shows a little cluster of houses in this area in 1784, and other sources suggest Joseph Gerrish may have built one or more houses here as early as 1760. However, a single sherd of creamware exposed in a tree throw at this site seemed a rather sparse verification—and time spent contemplating a "Holy Well," a natural spring framed by flat-laid stone (now all-too-visible after Juan), did not provide much inspiration.

Nevertheless, the natural disaster of Hurricane Juan—on the last day of fieldwork in the park—did provide an unprecedented glimpse of Point Pleasant Park's history. During the final walkabout assessment just days before the park's eagerly anticipated reopening on June 4, 2004, one last discovery was made: in the vicinity of the glade, a well-preserved stone-lined well was found, buried in cut boughs, along with hints of foundation walls, more ceramics, and a lead musket ball. As so often happens in archaeology, the potential for further discoveries revealed itself most clearly at the very end of the project.

This story is dedicated to the memory of Colin Stewart: cyclist, biologist, and consultant to the Halifax Regional Municipality, who passed away during the restoration of his beloved Point Pleasant Park.

Deadmans Island
Preserving the Past for the Future

Michele Raymond
Member of the Legislative Assembly, Halifax Atlantic

Historical research can help pinpoint the location of hidden archaeological remains. If archaeologists do not investigate those remains right away, they can always investigate them in the future, as long as the remains are not destroyed. Knowing the archaeological value of a site, then, can (and ideally should) lead to its preservation for the future. A case in point is Deadmans Island, located on the mainland side of Halifax's Northwest Arm. Little archaeology has been done there, but historians have shown that the island's past makes it a promising candidate for future archaeology. Fortunately, destruction of its archaeological remains has been averted by a concerted effort of far-sighted citizens as well as the Halifax Regional Municipality and the American government.

In fact, "Deadmans Island" is a misnomer. Situated in a small cove near the head of the Northwest Arm, the land is actually a steep and stony wooded hill connected to the shore by a narrow isthmus, which is often washed over by spring tides. The cove is known as Melville Cove, and the only real island in it is Melville Island. It is Melville Island that has lent its notoriety to Deadmans.

The Northwest Arm is an integral, well-documented part of the story of Halifax. There have been no extensive archaeological excavations in the area, but maps, sketches, paintings, and diary entries produced over nearly 250 years have created an enviable basis for future archaeological investigations.

Images of the Northwest Arm are found worldwide; it has long been virtually a set piece for visiting artists. Melville Cove is one of the most picturesque spots along the Arm, and, as a military facility, it often drew the attention of military artists attached to the naval base at Halifax. Nova Scotia Archives and Records Management, Maritime Museum of the Atlantic, Maritime Museum at Norfolk, Public Records Office at Greenwich, Boston Public Library, and Pennsylvania Historical Society all contain documents with information about the past uses of the cove. Local folklore and occasional newspaper articles mention bones being exposed on Deadmans Island after storms or during garden work.

Early History

From the earliest days of the French–British struggle on the eastern seaboard of North America, Chibouctou (an early name for Halifax Harbour) attracted the attention of both powers. French fishing stations had been established early on McNabs Island near the mouth of the Arm but were pillaged by the British in 1688. The first British map of the area, prepared in 1732 by Admiral Durrell, is well known to historians for erroneously identifying the Arm as Hawkes or Sandwich River. When Cornwallis established temporary settlement at Sandwich Point (Point Pleasant) in 1749, investigations quickly showed that the river was actually a slender arm of the great harbour. Sandwich Point itself was too exposed to weather, so the settlement was moved into the lee of today's Citadel Hill. It

Opposite page: This 1801 watercolour by George I. Parkyns shows Melville Cove in the romantic light favoured by nineteenth-century artists at the Northwest Arm.

was also soon apparent that not all of the town's needs could be met on the peninsula. Water power and fresh running water to power mills were scarce there, and the soil was poor. Dartmouth proved more welcoming, but within three years, a few of the more ambitious settlers were also eyeing the far western shores of the Northwest Arm.

Robert Cowie and John Aubony were among these ambitious settlers. A baker and a tavern keeper in town, they applied for and jointly received a grant of 64.8 hectares at the head of the Arm. The island there became Cowie's Island, and the steep slopes of the shore behind it, Cowie's Hill. The name for the hill has persisted ever since.

The island first appears in the public media in 1752, when Cowie and Aubony, having built a storage shed and fortified blockhouse, advertised the complex in the *Halifax Gazette* as an ideal site for a shingle mill. It was never used as a shingle mill, but it was developed as a fishing station by the next landowner, James Kavanagh. In the eighteenth century, the Arm was a rich fishery, and well into the twentieth century it yielded ample mackerel, cod, clams, and lobster, as well as the occasional shark.

Kavanagh and his family lived on the island until 1803, when the Napoleonic Wars had so overfilled the floating prison hulks anchored in Bedford Basin that the Admiralty was forced to seek prison space.

Ten years earlier, Lieutenant Governor John Wentworth had proposed renting the island to house French prisoners away from the diseases of town. Only in 1803, however, did the Admiralty finally use the island as a prison, first renting it and then purchasing all of Kavanagh's land, renaming the island "Melville," in honour of the first Lord of Admiralty, Viscount Melville. Naval authorities refurbished Kavanagh's house and constructed a wooden prison. A persistent rumour claims that the prison warden's house (today's Armdale Yacht Clubhouse), built in 1809, was brought from Pictou (at present, there is no way to prove or disprove this assertion).

MELVILLE ISLAND PRISONS Melville Island, located in the Northwest Arm of Halifax, was purchased by the British in 1804 for use as a prison, and named after the Lord of the Admiralty, Viscount Melville. A tiny island with a formidable prison structure, this was an effective jail for the thousands of prisoners-of-war (POWs) unfortunate enough to end up there, especially if, as Thomas Raddall claimed, prison guards told inmates that the waters surrounding the island were shark-infested. Prisoner diaries report that the island's inmates kept themselves busy in many ways, keeping animals and producing crafts like small ship models made from bone, which they sold to fashionable Haligonians. Many POWs from the Napoleonic Wars, the War of 1812, British military prisoners, and even German prisoners from World War One served time on the island. Those who died were buried on a small, adjacent tip of land aptly called Deadmans Island. The main prison buildings were ravaged by fire in 1935, and in 1945, the military presence left the island; it was then leased to the Armdale Yacht Club. –SM

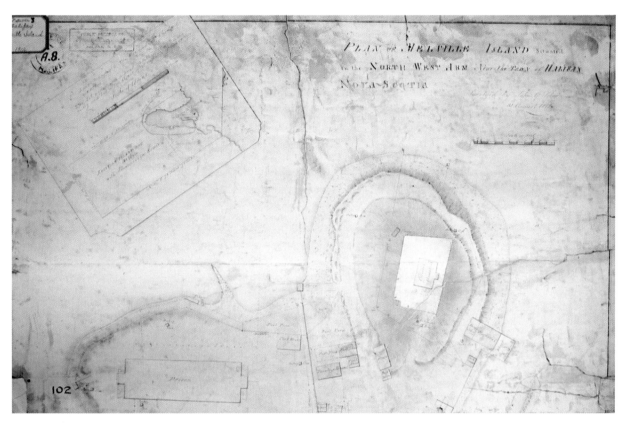

This 1812 map of Melville Island by John George Toler pinpoints various facilities on the prison island. There is a wharf at the hospital, opposite Deadmans Island. Prison diaries refer to the dead being rowed across the cove for burial.

The prison building is described in great detail by François Lambert Bourneuf, a French prisoner who escaped twice (once successfully). Escapes were frequent, particularly after prisoners and guards had gone drinking together off the island. Bourneuf's diary depicts a rather charming coexistence of keepers and the kept and a complicated economy in which prisoners and guards collaborated to provide luxury goods, dancing lessons, and trinkets for visiting British officers and their wives. Some of these trinkets, including carved bone spoons and at least one silk-rigged model ship, are still found in a few Halifax households.

The complexion of life on the island changed radically with the War of 1812. Many French prisoners were put out on parole to outlying communities, and the prison land was quickly jammed with American captives, mostly young privateers who had set sail from New England ports to make their fortunes at sea. At one point, more than sixteen hundred prisoners were crowded into the prisoners' half of the 1.6-hectare island. Prisoners' particulars at Halifax were recorded in prisoner rolls. The roll called "French and Americans at Halifax: Died, Run, Retaken" is a treasure trove of information, and, in combination with the diaries of American prisoners, tells us why the soil of Deadmans Island is filled with bones.

John G. Toler's 1812 map of the prison facility marks a hospital, and beside it a wharf facing south towards what we call Deadmans Island. Between 1812 and 1814 the hospital wharf saw 188 American prisoners cast off for the last time, bound for burial in the wooded knoll. "Four prisoners carried today to Target Hill, a place where they bury the dead," comments the diary of Massachusetts prisoner Benjamin Palmer, referring to Deadmans Island.

The closing months of the War of 1812 saw many Southern slaves escape to the shores of Chesapeake Bay, where they sought sanctuary with the British, who brought them to Nova Scotia. When smallpox broke out at Halifax in 1815, the refugees were vaccinated and moved out to Melville Island for their own safety, staying in abandoned prison buildings that were hastily whitewashed and repaired, according to account books at Nova Scotia Archives and Records Management. There are also accounts of the hearty provisions (beef, beer, bread, potatoes, rice, molasses, Indian meal, and coffee) and clothing issued to the refugees. Despite the removal, at least 104 refugees died and

Interior of old detention barracks, 1929.

presumably were buried on Target Hill. The island fell into disuse once the refugees moved onto their land grants, although a few families settled along Melville Island Road and at the head of the Arm. In 1829, Thomas Chandler Haliburton described the picturesque ruins:

> There are about ten buildings upon it, which, together with a garden, nearly cover its surface. The principal one is the prison, a long wooden house, two stories in height, whose grated windows bespeak the use to which it has been applied. All the buildings are in a state of neglect and decay; a wooden bridge connects the Island with the main land, and on a small hill to the southward is the burying ground belonging to the establishment. It is now no longer to be distinguished from the surrounding woods, but by the mounds of earth which have been placed over the dead; the whole being covered with a thick shrubbery of forest trees. (22)

The island remained deserted until the potato famine brought shiploads of Irish immigrants to town, many ill with typhus fever. Once again, Melville Island was pressed into service as a quarantine station. At least thirty Irish immigrants died there in the summer of 1847, and they were apparently buried on Target Hill. They were probably the last burials from Melville Island. And Melville Island was used again in 1851, to briefly house Foreign Legion recruits that Joseph Howe rounded up in the United States.

Flogging and hanging had long been the punishments for deserters from the British forces, and in 1854, when the British army abolished these practices, it suddenly found itself in need of more prison space. Melville Island was transferred to the army in 1856, and for the next fifty years it housed military deserters and other miscreants.

The Twentieth Century

The stone cells that most people think of as the Melville Island prison were built around 1905. The following year, the British forces left Canada for good, and Melville Island, along with all the other British military properties, was transferred to the Canadian government. The complex was used for Canadian army prisoners until 1909.

By this time, the shores of Melville Cove were already becoming a popular summer resort area. The Hosterman family, longtime owners of the mills at the head of the Arm, had earlier turned some of their lands into Hosterman's Pleasure Grounds. To the south, Charles Longley had set up his own pleasure grounds, which included a dance hall and boathouse on Deadmans Island. (Longley may have been the person to give the island its name, since, when he found skulls in the garden, he began using them as decoration in his dance hall.)

German prisoners of war were held on Melville Island during World War One, but the island was never again used as a prison. On the eve of World War Two, in 1935, the old wooden cells burned. The island served as an ammunition depot for a brief period during the war, but the residents of the significant cottage colony that had developed at the cove objected, and the military materiel was removed.

The recreational potential of the Northwest Arm was enormous, and at the end of World War Two, the Department of National Defense leased Melville Island to the Armdale Yacht Club, which had been perched on the northern shore of the cove. The club has adapted the stone cells as storage lockers and added decks to the warden's house, but the distinctive roofline from 1805 remains a landmark on the Arm, and the upstairs fireplaces and some of the early hardware on doors in the basement and attic help tell the story of what is probably the oldest building on the Arm today.

Deadmans Preserved

Thousands of people now live willingly at Melville Cove. Regatta Point was developed on the former Hosterman's Pleasure Grounds (and Edmonds Grounds) in the 1980s, and in 1998, a proposal was put forward to build condominiums on Deadmans Island. (A 1973 proposal for a highrise had been rejected, but so was an application for heritage

Melville Island Military Prison, in 1929.

designation.) The 1998 plan was to hollow out the hill for a parking garage and place a sixty-unit building on top.

A Northwest Arm Heritage Association had existed intermittently, under various names, for more than thirty years, and once again the group sprang into action. "Why is it called Deadmans?" they asked, and quickly began to compile a wealth of historical information about Deadmans Island and adjacent areas. The information included documents from Nova Scotia Archives and Records Management, paintings and maps from around the world, written stories of life and death on Melville Island, and diaries and newspaper articles about the burials, bones, and musket balls on Target Hill. Archaeologist Laird Niven conducted a survey of Deadmans Island that appeared to confirm that the burials were still there.

Armed with all this information, the association alerted the public and multiple levels of government to the significance of Deadmans. The *New York Times*, *Boston Globe*, and *Globe and Mail*, as well as the American government, all acknowledged its significance. In 2000, responding to this campaign, the Halifax Regional Municipality decided to purchase Deadmans for preservation and incorporation into its system of parks. In 2005, the US government intends to erect a memorial to the soldiers and sailors buried there; French, Spanish, Irish, and African-American burials will also be memorialized. Nosadmans Island is preserved, its archaeological remains (if not the burials themselves) can be explored in the future, if desired.

Along the Shubenacadie Canal

Stephen A. Davis, Saint Mary's University
April D. MacIntyre, Memorial University of Newfoundland

THE HISTORY OF THE SHUBENACADIE CANAL watershed as a transport route dates back thousands of years. The 115-kilometre system of rivers and lakes cuts across Nova Scotia, and was a well-travelled highway for First Nations people between Halifax Harbour and the Bay of Fundy—with long periods of clear navigation and relatively few portages—for generations before the arrival of Europeans.

After the founding of Halifax in 1749, the military and commercial value of the waterway was not lost on the new settlement. As it was, reaching the Bay of Fundy meant sailing around the southern tip of the province at Cape Sable, a treacherous route. As the late eighteenth century was a period of intensive canal building in Great Britain, it is not surprising that plans to adapt the Shubenacadie waterway for uninterrupted navigation gained increasing currency.

While the Shubenacadie Canal ultimately enjoyed a very short period of operation—much shorter than the troubled history of its construction—it stands today as a remarkable and little-known chapter in the archaeological record of the province.

THE CANAL AGE (1760–1840) Among the many by-products of the Industrial Revolution that began to transform Great Britain in the mid-eighteenth century was what is now referred to as the Canal Age. With the increased and widespread demand for coal to power steam engines, the construction of inland waterways emerged as a faster and less expensive means of transporting freight, in contrast to the rutted and meandering system of roads. Between 1760 and 1800, a frenzy of construction (and technical innovation) produced more than fifty canals, constituting over six thousand kilometres of waterway which linked Britain as never before. While this enthusiasm for canal building carried over to North America, by the start of the nineteenth century it was already on the decline in Britain. By 1840 many British canals were falling into disrepair, as their status had been eclipsed by the ascension of the railway. –RP

History of the Canal

It was in 1824 that the dream of constructing a canal system on the Shubenacadie waterway began to take shape. On July 25, 1826, Lord Dalhousie, Governor General of British North America, turned the first sod at a ceremony at Port Wallace, in what is now Shubie Park in Dartmouth. Designed after the British style, the canal plans called for a total of seventeen stone locks: seven on the steep ascent from Halifax Harbour to Lake Banook and ten on the long descent from Lake Charles to Minas Basin, on the Bay of Fundy. A channel had to be cut through the 1.4 kilometres of land separating Lake Charles and Lake Micmac (including a "deep cut" through 1.2 metres of bedrock), and two locks were to be constructed in this section.

Opposite page: An American-style lock built during the second construction phase, 1831-1854.

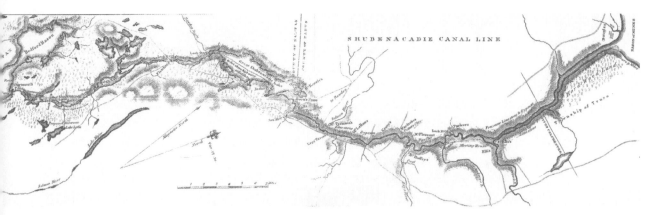

Francis Hall's 1826 plan for the construction of the Shubenacadie Canal.

Charles R. Fairbanks

The construction of the canal went on year round, with up to three hundred labourers and specialists employed in the summer. Slightly fewer men were employed in the winter months to quarry stone and transport it to the lock sites. In order to provide skilled granite workers, a ship was sent to Scotland to bring back forty-four masons and stone cutters, their families, and tonnes of stone. Carpenters, axemen, mechanics, blacksmiths, and limeburners (who made lime by burning limestone or shells) were also engaged in the construction of the waterway.

Work progressed without incident until 1829, when planner Francis Hall reported to the Shubenacadie Canal Company that the total expense of the project would exceed the estimated cost by twenty-two thousand pounds. The company, then in dire financial straits, sent its secretary, Charles R. Fairbanks, to England to obtain a loan from the British government. By obtaining the loan and selling shares, Fairbanks managed to raise sufficient funds for work on the canal to continue. In spite of increased capital, however, additional construction and repairs necessitated by the harsh Nova Scotian winter came at a time when the company could ill afford them. On November 20, 1831, the workers, who had been paid only sporadically since August, walked off the job. Thirteen of the proposed seventeen locks were in various stages of completion, but work had not yet begun on the Dartmouth Harbour facilities or on the Shubenacadie River, making only short sections of the canal navigable.

The death of C. R. Fairbanks resulted in foreclosures by both his executors and the British government, who held the mortgage on the canal works and property. For two decades, the most ambitious engineering project the province had ever seen was at a standstill. At last the province of Nova Scotia obtained the assets of the Shubenacadie Canal Company, and in 1853 the canal was purchased by the newly formed Inland

Navigation Company, of which C. W. Fairbanks was chief engineer. Fairbanks revised the original canal plans to eliminate eight locks by the addition of two inclined planes (also known as marine railways), at Dartmouth Cove and Portobello. After the American style, Fairbanks also declared the locks should be built of wood and domestic stone—a solution at once cheaper and more suited to the climate (the use of imported stone that

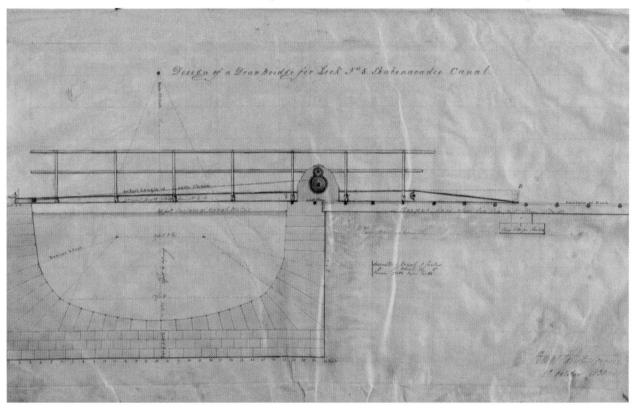

An illustration of the draw-bridge for a lock along the canal.

cracked with the cold had led to costly repairs). The new company managed to complete seven locks and the marine railway at Portobello under this new scheme before its funds were exhausted and work ceased once more. In the spring of 1860, the company mortgaged the canal properties and land. Angus McDougall, former assistant engineer to Fairbanks, was appointed chief engineer, and construction began on the Dartmouth marine railway. Finally, in the summer of 1861, the steamer *Avery* travelled the full length of the Shubenacadie Canal from Halifax Harbour to Maitland and back—thirty-five years after construction on the canal had begun.

However, the ghost of financial ruin that hung over the canal still haunted the Inland Navigation Company, and despite efforts to improve its financial condition, the company property and canal works were seized and sold at a sheriff's auction on June 11, 1862. They were purchased by the newly founded Lake and River Navigation Company, which operated three steamboats (*Mayflower*, *Lilly*, and *Avery*), twelve scows,

*Lewis P.
Fairbanks*

and an eighty-tonne barge. These vessels carried bricks and pottery, as well as logs and squared timber, from the head of the Shubenacadie River to Halifax. On the return trip, they carried supplies to the new gold mining operations in Waverley.

Profits from the canal were not as high as expected, however, and on April 1, 1870, the Lake and River Navigation Company accepted an offer from Lewis P. Fairbanks, brother of C. W. Fairbanks, for the canal works and properties. Shortly after acquiring the canal, L. P. Fairbanks was faced with an insurmountable obstruction to canal navigation. The provincially owned Nova Scotia Railway built a deck truss span on its bridge over the canal at Enfield, and the province replaced a drawbridge over the canal at Waverley with a fixed bridge. It thereby became impossible for steamboats to navigate the Shubenacadie Canal, and the canal ceased to exist as a commercial waterway.

Archaeology of the Canal

Archaeological investigation of the Shubenacadie Canal began in the fall of 1983, when Public Works Canada awarded a six-week contract to Saint Mary's University. This initial contract was granted to "assist in the identification of heritage resources within a restricted area of the Shubenacadie Canal system," with the study area defined as that which now encompasses Shubie Park at Port Wallace. The investigation included an intensive walking survey of the study area, as well as archival research.

The results of the investigation led to the discovery of nineteen heritage features, including several foundations of varying sizes and representing a range of construction techniques. The foundations were overgrown with trees predating the twentieth century, and many of the features had clearly been disturbed by campers and visitors to the park, as well as by the modern upgrade of the trail system. Only two of these features—remains of a blacksmith's shop and a lockkeeper's house—could be positively identified in contemporary written accounts as relating to the canal. Fifteen of the remaining heritage features (including a hunter's blind, portions of canal walls, a stone culvert, and old roadways) were believed to be associated with the canal construction and operation, while the remaining two were identified as pre-(European) contact, First Nations encampments.

A second archaeology contract came later that year from the Nova Scotia Department of Development to investigate the area that is now the site of the Canal Interpretation Centre, located at the corner of Alderney Drive and Portland Street on the Dartmouth waterfront. As in the first investigation, archaeologists were directed to determine the potential of the area to provide information on heritage features. Over the years, extensive waterfront development had led to massive alterations to the landscape, primarily during deposition of landfill to provide a deep anchorage for the Dartmouth Marine Slips. These site alterations necessitated adjustments to the investigative methodology, with the result that subsurface testing occurred both manually and with the aid of backhoes.

The excavation of Wellington Lock, 1989. Submerged in water is the mitre sill, the abutment against which sat the bottom of the canal gate.

While archival research identified twelve potential occupants and industries within or near the study area (including the Dartmouth Lumber Company, Hartshorne/Tremaine Gristmill, Nantucket Whaling Company, James Settle's Blacksmith Shop, and the Town of Dartmouth stonecrusher, among other mills, shipyards, and structures related to the canal), subsurface testing failed to reveal evidence of any of the these occupants or industries. It did, however, lead to the discovery of a mysterious wall buried roughly a metre underground at the north end of the Dartmouth Shipyard. This wall was 20.0 metres long and 2.2 metres high and had been constructed using a dry-wall technique. No archival evidence could be found to identify it, and the function of the wall remains as yet unknown, although it has been suggested that the wall is linked to the first phase of canal construction.

In 1984, Public Works Canada provided additional funds to conduct the mitigation plan proposed in the first report on the canal. Mitigation involves minimizing the impact of development on archaeological resources. This particular mitigation plan called for an extensive archival background study as well as selective testing and excava-

An excavated residence, 1984. This residence was probably built by Irish immigrants who came to work on the canal during its first construction phase, 1831-1854. The building is reminiscent of traditional residences then found in Ireland and Scotland.

tion of the features at Shubie Park recorded during the first phase of the investigation. The fieldwork component consisted of four months of excavation followed by four months of analysis. The excavations concentrated on five locations thought to contain features related to canal construction activities, which the ground surface suggested were a blacksmith's shop, a black powder magazine, a stone-cutting area, a dwelling, and a small structure thought to be a hunter's blind (probably post-dating operation of the canal).

A Surprising Discovery

On the basis of excavated evidence it seems that the dwelling had been a residence for one or two families. It was known through archival research that the Shubenacadie Canal Company did provide housing for its navvies, or workers, and an early map of the canal placed a workers' camp on the high ground at the east side of lock number three. (Locks number two and three are both located in what is now Shubie Park, where the 1.4-kilometre "deep cut" was made to allow passage from Lake Micmac to Lake Charles.) However, the dwelling in question would have stood apart from the workers' camp, and so its discovery had been a surprise in the initial archaeological survey.

Excavation of this residence revealed a double-skinned, dry-stone-walled structure with most of three walls toppled inwards. Its interior living space would have measured

7.9 by 3.4 metres. The construction of the residence employed a natural feature of the site, in that its northeast wall had been set into a large bank of soil. This wall was the least preserved, as it had been built using only a single layer of stone. A combination of tree root activity and frost had caused it to collapse. The wall had two obvious hearths, one of which had a well laid flagstone floor. The opposite wall contained the only access to the residence—a narrow doorway preceded by a flagstone walkway. Before excavation, a large spruce tree was removed from the entrance. This tree had ninety annual growth rings, indicating that the site had been abandoned at least ninety years earlier. The same wall that once accommodated the entrance also produced the only evidence of a window—a small quantity of plate window glass was found scattered on top of the wall to the east of the door. Excavation of the interior of the residence also revealed that

LOCKS AND PLANES One essential technical problem to be overcome in order for canals to be built over great distances, across uneven terrain: how to make water run uphill. Accordingly, while the history of the canal stretches back thousands of years, its modern usage dates to the middle ages and the invention of the canal lock to address this very problem.

By the eighteenth century, lock design had come to consist of a water-tight chamber linking sections of canal built at different heights. For instance, if a boat entered the lock from the higher section of canal, the gates would close behind it, then water would be drained until it reached the level of the lower section, at which time the other set of gates would open and the boat would continue on its course. In situations where the canal had to make a steep ascent, a series of staircase locks would be built in sequence.

The inclined plane (or marine railway) was invented as an alternative to the costly and time-consuming process of building multiple locks. A skid attached to a winch would be lowered into position underneath the boat at the bottom of the plane, then the boat would be simply hauled up the incline (by a water-driven turbine), to be set back in the water at the top and continue along the canal. –RP

the floor was made of hard-packed earth laid over naturally occurring layers of stone, a design that would have afforded excellent drainage.

It was clear that the residence had been constructed after the canal bed was dug. Naturally, blasting during excavation for the canal would have provided readily available building material. The lowest courses of stone within the foundation as well as the remaining walls bore angular fractures, resulting from blasting, which confirmed their origin. Furthermore, the northeast wall had been set into a linear pile of stones discarded from the canal construction.

Typically in archaeological excavations of nineteenth-century residences, homes once sheltered by a planked or shingled roof are distinguished by the presence of large quantities

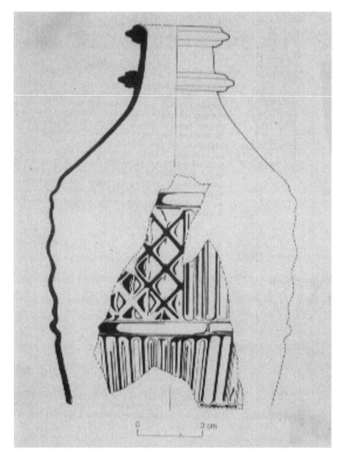

A bottle "reconstructed" from a single fragment, which was collected from the residence excavated in 1984 and dates to the early nineteenth century.

of nails scattered throughout the interior. The only nails recovered from this residence were found around the entrance and in the hearths. This distribution implies that the dwelling had a framed door and that the occupants were burning scrap wood in the hearths. Also typically in excavations of nineteenth-century residences, the presence of a drip line along the walls implies that the roof extended past the walls. No drip line was present here. The inference, then, is that the residence did not have a planked or shingled roof and that the roof did not extend past the walls.

Ceramics and bottle glass excavated from inside the residence date to the first half of the nineteenth century. This artifactual evidence, combined with the fact that the residence was built of stone blasted from the canal, suggests that the residence was occupied for a brief period of time at or near the end of the first canal building phase, around 1830. The occupants left no evidence that they were other than humble folk, possibly workers who chose not to live in the company houses provided for them. Given the extensive documentary record of the canal at Nova Scotia Archives

and Records Management, the research team expected that it would be a straightforward (although time-consuming) task to identify the occupants of the house and other canal workers, possibly by name. Researcher Bill Russell conducted an exhaustive search at the archives but, surprisingly, discovered little more than the following description by William Moorsom:

A village of the most primitive description has gradually risen around the principle [sic] point of operations, about three miles from Dartmouth: the first huts were constructed with logs, loose stones and mud, roofed with boughs and rough strips of bark, and their very existence was scarce discoverable till you almost stumbled over them. Every summer a shade of improvement has become visible. The principle [sic] cabin; or that where liquor is retailed, was originally distinguished by a long pole planted in front of the door, like those which in Canada designate the residence of a captain of militia. Latterly, this tenement has assumed the aspect of a little tavern, neatly boarded on the outside, and capable of affording what we still see expressed on some out-of-the-way country signs as "entertainment for man and horse." The inhabitants of this village and of other cabins scattered along the line are Irish emigrants, who land without a shilling in their pockets and here find immediate employment. (325–326)

At least for the time being, the identities of the Shubenacadie Canal workers who resided in the excavated dwelling remain unknown.

The Canal at Portobello

The archaeological rescue of the canal from obscurity and decay continued in 2003, when the Shubenacadie Canal Commission awarded a contract to Davis Archaeological Consultants Limited to investigate several features in the area of Portobello, at the north end of Lake Charles. Included in the study were a masonry dam, the inclined plane designed by C. W. Fairbanks, and a lock that was later converted to a waste weir. Archaeologists conducted detailed historical and archival research and made contacts with canal and inclined plane experts in Canada, the United States, and the United Kingdom. Field investigations focused primarily on cleaning and assessing the present state of features within the study area as part of a development scheme to make the canal navigable by canoe.

Elements of the canal complex at Portobello had long eluded discovery. After its abandonment in 1870, this site—like all the main features of the canal—was dismantled and the parts salvaged for scrap. The removal of features such as the lock gates and the turbine that once powered the marine railway at Portobello left no surface evidence to study. Complicating matters further, no plans for the construction of the inclined plane and lock have survived.

In 2003, fieldwork and related documentary research shed light on much of the history of this section of the canal. Even so, questions remain. At the base of the masonry dam is a stone-lined drain that leads away from the dam toward a secondary drain. This configuration has never been explained by canal experts, but efforts are now being made to under-stand the role it played in the operation of the canal. It appears that the lock, which was later converted to a waste weir, went through several episodes of reconstruction and repair. Fortunately, the gate niches on the lock walls and the adjacent sluice culverts—built to raise and lower water levels in the lock—remain in very good condition.

A circular drain in the masonry dam at Portobello. The drain may be related to the operation of a water turbine, which pulled boats up and down the inclined plane between Lake Charles and Lake William.

Archaeological investigations at Portobello are on-going and, with any luck, this section of the storied Shubenacadie Canal will eventually be restored for all to enjoy.

Preservation and Restoration

Today, twenty years after archaeological study of the Shubenacadie Canal began, Nova Scotia's largest watershed is enjoying renewed interest—for its natural beauty as well as its history. The waterway is a popular destination for canoeing and kayaking, and has hosted international competitions for these sports. Furthermore, the efforts of the Canal Commission have led to the development of an extensive hiking trail system and the restoration of several sections of the canal. Once nearly forgotten, this singular engineering achievement has finally received the recognition it deserves.

The archaeology of the Shubenacadie Canal has filled in many gaps in the documented

history of an engineering marvel. Archaeology along the canal has delved into the lives of the Irish navvies responsible for building the canal and, in turn, opened up an aspect of the history of the canal that otherwise would probably remain unknown. It has also enhanced our understanding of some canal construction and operational elements. Perhaps most importantly, archaeology along the Shubenacadie canal has resulted in the restoration of many portions of the canal as well as the designation of part of it (Fletcher's Lock) as a Special Place under the provincial *Special Places Protection Act*. The Shubenacadie Canal has claimed its rightful place as unique and innovative technology during the "canal mania" that swept across North America in the early nineteenth century.

The Fairbanks Interpretation Centre

Excavation of Seaview African United Baptist Church, Africville

Katie Cottreau-Robins, Saint Mary's University

The excavation of Seaview African United Baptist Church in Africville clearly shows how the field of archaeology is about making connections. By examining the physical remains of a site, archaeologists use these tangible links to the past to address important historical questions. Doing so provides extraordinary opportunities for physical, social, personal—even spiritual—connections. Urban archaeology, in particular, can benefit from such interactions, as it usually takes place in densely populated areas. The case study of the Seaview African United Baptist Church demonstrates the inherent connective quality of archaeology, highlighting the importance of collaboration in providing any genuine understanding of a past time and place.

The "God is Love" banner, an exciting discovery during excavation of the Seaview Church site.

Seaview Church

Africville was an African–Nova Scotian community settled around 1848 in the far north end of peninsular Halifax along the shoreline of Bedford Basin. The central institution in the community was the Seaview African United Baptist Church. The church was built after 1916 (fire destroyed an earlier church) along Campbell Road (predecessor of north Barrington Street), the main road through Africville. Spiritual and social life revolved around the church, with events such as baptisms, weddings, and funerals drawing community members together. One former resident recalls the annual Easter Sunday sunrise service:

> They went into the church singing spirituals, around four or five o'clock in the morning when the sun came up, and did not come out till three p.m....People, including Whites, used to come from miles around to the sunrise service, sometimes from Truro and New Glasgow and usually from Preston and Hammond's Plains. (in Clairmont, 40)

In the 1960s, Seaview Church was demolished along with the rest of Africville in a controversial episode of "urban renewal." Later, much of the site was converted into Seaview Park. Ever since, the church has been a focal point of efforts to keep the memory of Africville alive.

Church Site Threatened

Previous page: An Africville relocation meeting at Seaview Church.

In 1991, Nova Scotia Economic Development Minister Tom McInnis announced the realignment of a planned access road to Richmond Terminal and the Canadian National Railway (CNR) Intermodal Yard. Realignment shifted the planned road onto CNR property in the vicinity of Seaview Park, where both the road and its landscape buffer would encroach on the site of Seaview Church. In an effort to preserve the memory of

Archaeologists begin to excavate. Site assistants Ken Lee and Euan Mathieson excavate a long line of building remains in Trench C.

Trench C fully excavated with foundation features exposed for recording of structural details. Structural information gathered during the excavation was to be used in the design of a church replica.

Africville, the provincial government agreed to fund the research for and design and construction of a church replica to be built close to the original site. They convened a consultation committee consisting of representatives of government, the Africville Genealogy Society, and the Technical University of Nova Scotia (now DalTech). The committee decided that the first order of business would be an archaeological excavation of the church site. Then a graduate student at the Technical University, I directed the excavation, which occupied four weeks during October and November 1992. The excavation team included crew members Ken Lee and Euan Mathieson and volunteer students from Saint Mary's University and Halifax West High School.

Excavating the Site

The plan was to use information obtained in the excavation to design a church replica, so locating and uncovering the church foundation became the main objective. Prior to excavation, the team determined the general location of the church through archival research, notably maps and photographs, and conversations with former Africville residents. They set up a key point of reference, a fourteen-metre east–west baseline, along the southern boundary of the church site. Then they cleared away surface debris and vegetation and prepared a contour map. A walking survey of the site proved helpful, because edges of foundation slabs were found just above the ground surface. The team decided that creating trenches to be excavated by shovel and trowel would be the most effective method of exposing the foundation. Four such trenches, ranging from seven to thirteen metres in length, were created.

Archaeology students from Halifax West High School.

Excavating in the trenches soon uncovered foundation sections and other structural features of the church. All but one section had been pulled up and pushed over during demolition. Foundation slabs often covered the entire width of the trenches, making digging cumbersome and labour-intensive. This is where the student volunteers from Halifax West High School proved especially helpful. For two days, working in groups of twenty-five, students excavated the associated rubble and soil. Working with these students was rewarding. They enjoyed the opportunity to participate in a hands-on learning experience and practise their digging techniques. They learned about Africville, and the pivotal role archaeology can play in the protection and management of heritage resources. At the same time, the archaeologists benefitted from much-needed extra hands and an energetic, youthful group eager to participate in discovering the past.

The archaeologists uncovered seven structural features: three fragmented walls, a foundation corner section, a chimney, and two foundation sections with openings for windows. The corner was the only section of the foundation relatively undisturbed and

BLACK SETTLEMENT IN NOVA SCOTIA In the mid-1700s, the population of Nova Scotia's blacks ranged from about fifty to a hundred, made up of mostly immigrants from New England who sought freedom (the total provincial population was 13,374). The late 1700s saw two major influxes of black settlers: the freed blacks from America and Maroons from Jamaica. During the American War of Independence, colonists who chose to side with Britain—the Loyalists—fled to Canada. Britain promised freedom from slavery to the black Loyalists; as a result, about ten percent of the refugees in Nova Scotia were black. In 1792, a significant number of the black Loyalists left in a major organized exodus for Sierra Leone. The Maroons were free blacks from Jamaica who had struggled for independence from colonial rule: about six hundred came to Nova Scotia between the years 1796 to 1800, primarily to work for the military. However, the poor treatment the Maroons received at the hands of the British caused them to seek new settlement. Most of the Maroons relocated to Sierra Leone. A significant migration of blacks to Nova Scotia came after the War of 1812 between Britain and America, resulting in about two thousand refugees from the United States. The British assured the escaped American slaves they would provide passage, land, and freedom. Such promises failed to fully materialize, however, as the former slaves encountered discrimination from the Nova Scotian government. Despite hardships, the immigrants' tenacity to survive won out, and black Nova Scotians formed deep-rooted settlements by the early 1800s, mostly in Hammonds Plains and Preston, though also in smaller pockets throughout the province. By 1850, the population of black Nova Scotians was nearly five thousand. –SM

Brick debris zone. Remains of the collapsed chimney from the Seaview Church.

A collection of blue and white labelled soda pop bottles was excavated from Trench F. The labels read "Arctic High Quality Beverage." The soda was manufactured by the Arctic Beverage Company in Halifax.

Fine tea wares. Archaeologists were not surprised to collect fragments of a decorated teapot, considering that Seaview Church was the location of many community gatherings.

still in its original position. This was significant, because it showed the geographical orientation of the church. Another interesting feature was the chimney and an associated zone of debris that, once analyzed, indicated how the building had collapsed during demolition. All of this architectural information, combined with historical information, can be used to design a church replica.

The stratigraphy of the site, comprising its superimposed archaeological layers, was similar from trench to trench. After a layer of sod was removed, a layer of concrete would appear. Next came a layer concentrated with building artifacts, such as wood, roofing, window glass, chimney

Africville before relocation

THE HISTORY OF AFRICVILLE Africville was a Nova Scotia black settlement with a highly publicized history. Known also as Campbell's Road or Seaview, its fifteen acres were located in the north end of Halifax peninsula near the Bedford Basin. The first blacks to come to Africville, mostly from Hammonds Plains and Preston, wanted to come closer to Halifax to find work in the city. The founders of the settlement were Willam Brown and William Arnold, who were granted deed to three five-acre lots, in 1848. Other families came to obtain smaller lots within these fifteen acres, and the settlement grew. Living conditions in Africville were challenging, without clean running water and the municipal services provided to other Halifax neighbourhoods. In the 1960s, the city controversially demolished the community, relocating the residents. –SM

liner, brick, stove pipe, nails, and spikes. This layer, called the "heavy debris zone," was clearly a record of the time of demolition and was helpful in determining the sequence of demolition events: First, the church superstructure was knocked down and debris filled the basement; then the foundation walls were pushed in and fell over the debris. Below the heavy debris zone was evidence of the concrete basement floor and footings.

The excavation yielded a total of 2,318 artifacts. When cleaned and identified, they turned out to represent four functional groups. The Domestic Artifact group comprised 1,289 artifacts related to personal and group activities, like clay smoking pipes, marbles, scissors, buttons, and fine and coarse ceramics. Additional artifacts in this category were coins, spoons, bottle glass, pliers, a lipstick holder, a toy wagon wheel, and a bottle opener. The Architectural Artifact group comprised 973 artifacts related to the church building, such as furnace grating, flashing, utility porcelain, window hardware, window glass, tile, bricks, nails, spikes, sheeting, staples, and light bulbs—plus hundreds of brick fragments. The Church Artifact group comprised 3 artifacts related to church activities, including a pair of wrist-length ladies' dress cotton gloves and a banner proclaiming "God is Love." The Miscellaneous Artifact group comprised 53 artifacts. One special artifact, which might someday be personally identified, was a copper alloy vendor's pin with the impression "REGISTER CHAUFFER 1919 2491 NOVA SCOTIA" and, on the back, "WELLINGS MFG. CO. TORONTO." Over seventy percent of these artifacts can be dated to the period of church use, from 1916 into the 1960s. A few exceptions—ceramics, bottle glass, and fragments of smoking pipes—predate the church period, according to their date of manufacture. These artifacts probably ended up at the site in landfill dumped there since demolition.

Accomplishments

After the excavation, immediately after archaeologists snapped a final photograph, a back-hoe moved in and bulldozed what remained of Seaview Church to make room for the realigned road. Everything was obliterated. Still, the main objective of the archaeological excavation was met. By locating, exposing, and studying the church foundation, archaeologists compiled information that can be used in designing the replica. They also amassed a

Archaeologists work side by side with heavy equipment and construction activity.

collection of artifacts associated with the church and its history, which is available for display, study, and recollection. The project was an encouraging example of urban archaeology in Halifax, because it afforded time for historical research, archaeological planning, and consultation with stakeholders. It also yielded information that could be incorporated into the social history of Africville.

At the time of the excavation, the plan was to complete the church replica before July 1993, the tenth anniversary of the formation of the Africville Genealogy Society and its annual Africville Reunion Weekend at Seaview Park. Since then, although the replica has surfaced in political discussions, its construction has not yet begun. The reasons are unclear. Its completion would be a moving tribute to Africville's memory.

Several organizations and individuals are responsible for success of the Seaview African United Baptist Church archaeology project: the Nova Scotia Department of Economic Development, which provided financial support; Parks Canada and DalTech, both of which provided equipment, laboratory space, and photographic and artifact conservation services; the Africville Genealogy Society, which provided support and historical information; Saint Mary's University and Halifax West High School, which provided student volunteers; Ken Lee and Euan Mathieson, who worked on the crew; Frank Eppell, who advised me in my role as project director; Irvine Carvery, who recalled living in Africville; and David Williamson, who helped to supervise the Halifax West student volunteers.

The Rockingham Inn Project

David Williamson, Halifax West High School

"Have I got an idea for you." With these words, an idea was born that grew to spark interest in local archeology in people of all ages and walks of life in Halifax. It was parents' night at Halifax West High School—where I taught an archaeology course—in February, 1994, and parent Glenn Taylor was speaking to me about his daughter. Taylor, past president of the Rockingham Heritage Society, was curious about a potential archaeological site in Rockingham, north of what is known locally as the Rotunda. More formally, the rotunda was the music room built on the estate of Prince Edward, Duke of Kent. Taylor's interest provided the seed of an idea that would eventually sprout into an intensive, two-week site excavation of the archeologically significant Rockingham Inn. Not only would this project highlight the cooperation between several diverse Halifax organizations, it would provide seventy-three students with an entirely new kind of education.

History of the Rockingham Inn

The Duke of Kent arrived in Halifax in 1794 and stayed with governor Sir John Wentworth. This arrangement was only temporary—soon Wentworth offered the duke use of his property on the shore of Bedford Basin, where he had a summer residence. By 1795–1796, the duke had built an estate on Wentworth's property that included a substantial home, numerous outbuildings, and a round music room. He also requested that his own regiment, the Royal Fusiliers, be stationed in Halifax under his command. The Fusiliers arrived in September 1795, and were housed on the nearby shore of the basin in several barracks, constructed for this purpose. They remained there until 1802.

Right: A painting of Governor Wentworth's estate, which became known as Prince's Lodge

Opposite page: The music room of Prince's Lodge, early 1900s

EDWARD AND JULIE Edward, Duke of Kent, built an expansive estate on the Bedford Basin waterfront for his mistress Julie St. Laurent. The only remnants of the estate are a round musical rotunda on the Basin, as well as the heart-shaped "Julie's Pond" at Hemlock Ravine in Rockingham. In 1800, Edward and Julie returned to England. Hemlock Ravine is now owned by the Halifax Regional Municipality and has a series of five interconnecting trails. –SM

Above: Prince Edward and Thérèse-Bernardine Mongenet, who was known as Julie and Madame de St. Laurent

When the duke left Halifax in 1800, the property was returned to Sir John Wentworth. Wentworth converted one of the barracks into a roadside inn, taking advantage of its strategic location along the highway (now the Bedford Highway) to Windsor. The inn, named the Rockingham Inn after a relative and patron, came to host the Rockingham Club, an exclusive social club that came to meet at the inn. This club included many of the most influential and prominent people in Halifax.

In 1810, when Wentworth returned to England, the inn property was sold to Robert Grovner. Although the Rockingham Club disbanded, a similar club, the Wellington

Club, took its place and also called the Rockingham Inn home. In 1815, the inn property was sold to David Muirhead and thereafter to several other owners. In 1833, tragedy struck as the Rockingham Inn was destroyed in a fire of unknown origin. A contemporary account of the catastrophe gives some details:

> On the night of Thursday last, that fine building known all over the country as the Rockingham Inn, was destroyed by fire. It originated in the stables adjoining which, with some cattle in it was nearly destroyed before the alarm was given. The wind being high, it was impossible for the few persons on the spot to prevent the flames from spreading to the dwelling house....The Rockingham being six miles from Town, no effectual assistance could be given, but a party of artillery persevered in dragging an engine as far as Birch Cove, and several officers and persons from the town reached the spot only in time to witness, but not mitigate the calamity. (in Williams)

After the 1833 fire, the property fell into disrepair and changed ownership several more times. Eventually, the once-proud Rockingham Inn was all but forgotten.

Archaeology Plans

In the 1990s, the Rockingham Heritage Society began monitoring the site of the Rockingham Inn. They feared that as the nearby shoreline eroded, the inn's remains might be exposed and washed into Bedford Basin. With this in mind, Glenn Taylor wondered if perhaps an archaeology class at Halifax West High School would conduct an excavation to recover and document the inn's remains. It was clear that professional archaeologists would have to be involved—legally, an individual cannot simply go to an archaeological site and start digging. Recovering an archeological site is a long, involved process, which begins with determining land ownership and obtaining research permits. Despite this, the Rockingham Inn site presented too many features of interest to not pursue the project. From a partially visible outer stone foundation or wall, to a scattering of bricks that appeared extremely old, a brief cursory survey revealed that this site presented an excellent opportunity to involve students in an important and exciting archaeology project.

Currently, only four Nova Scotian high schools teach a distinct archaeology course, which was developed by three Halifax teachers: William Fougere, Carmon Stone, and myself. Since the inception of the course in 1985, high school students have participated in several archaeological activities in Halifax; projects on Citadel Hill and in former Africville at the site of the former Seaview African United Baptist Church proved that high school students are fully capable of working alongside professional archaeologists. In these earlier activities, however, the students had simply worked for several days and then returned to class. Nothing on the scale of what was being proposed for the Rockingham Inn—a project spanning several weeks—had ever been attempted by a Halifax high school class before.

Opposite: The Rockingham Inn site before excavation.

With support from the Nova Scotia Archaeology Society and local government officials, the obstacles to finding professional help and funding were soon overcome. Paul Williams, president of the Nova Scotia Archaeology Society at the time, volunteered to direct the excavation, a commitment that required many weeks on his part. Williams enlisted the services of professional volunteers from the Canadian Parks Service and Saint Mary's University, and a valuable grant was obtained from the Nova Scotia Museum (the project was later awarded a provincial Hilroy Fellowship for curriculum development).

Involving students in an intensive, long-term excavation project raised numerous practical questions. What if students were injured? How would students make up for lost class time? How would classes be handled if there was a cancellation? The team decided to involve the seventy-three students in the Halifax West archaeology course in groups of about fifteen, with each group working for two days. This plan was manageable and ensured that the students did not miss a large amount of instructional time in their other courses.

Top: Halifax West High School students begin work in grids marked by string and stakes.

Bottom: An excavated corner of the Rockingham Inn. Once exposed, the rough courses of stone are conspicuous.

The Dig

The big day arrived on Monday, October 3, 1994. (To prepare the area, however, members of the archaeology society had spent the previous two weekends clearing vegetation off the site.) The day turned out to be unseasonably cold, with the temperature hitting a bone-chilling two degrees Celsius and with a strong north wind blowing off Bedford Basin. To their credit, the first fifteen students came dressed for the weather and, despite the cold, listened eagerly to the instructions given to them by their supervisors.

And so the adventure began. Most of the first two days consisted of hard labour, breaking through the top soil with little to show for the effort. The students were not discouraged, despite their enthusiasm to find artifacts. By the end of the second day, five excavation pits had been opened, and a potential foundation stone was beginning to be revealed. As luck would have it, on the third day, just as the students were getting into some serious excavation, the weather broke, and conditions became summer-like. Who could ask for more?

For the next two weeks, the students became archaeologists. When Howard Carter was asked what he saw when he first peered into the tomb of Tutankhamen, he reportedly said, "I see wonderful things" (35). The student archeological team experienced similar

Top: Archaeologist Paul Williams supervises students who have excavated one pit to a modest depth.

Bottom: Trays of artifacts recovered from the Rockingham Inn site awaiting further study at Saint Mary's University.

Right: Laboratory analysis. Parks Canada researcher Janet Stoddard supervises students drawing cleaned potsherds in a biology laboratory at Halifax West High School.

wonder as the foundation of the structure began to be exposed. By the end of the ten-day excavation, the team had uncovered parts of the east and west walls of the Rockingham Inn, its kitchen or pantry, a possible garbage pit, and a porch or veranda facing Bedford Basin. The outline and orientation of the building were now clear. The list of recovered artifacts was eclectic: a watch chain, door knob, lock plate, pipe bowl, gaming tokens, buttons, melted window glass, square roofing nails, sherds of Chinese porcelain, and more sherds of ceramic creamware and pearlware.

While the excitement of discovering artifacts was the students' high point, the unearthing of the foundation and evidence of a major fire proved most interesting to the professional archaeologists. Research had revealed that the Rockingham Inn was destroyed by a major fire in 1833. An excavated layer of charcoal, scorched pottery sherds, and melted window glass supported that information. Combined with the additional discovery of a Royal Fusilier military uniform button, the team knew it had found the searched-for inn. But time was running out, because the students had to return to their regular classes. After the students' direct involvement was over, Williams and the other archaeologists spent the last days on the site completing their work. The final, arduous task required back-filling the excavation. (Back-filling involves lining an excavation with plastic and then re-filling it with excavated dirt, protecting the excavation and facilitating the resumption of digging at a later date.)

The Rockingham Inn project did not end with the last shovel of dirt. Before going into the field, the team had planned to conduct several laboratory sessions with the students once the excavation was completed. These sessions were arranged and carried out by volunteers from the Canadian Parks Service in the biology laboratories at Halifax West. In the laboratories, the students learned how to clean, identify, catalogue, and conserve a variety of the artifacts discovered. The students then began working on a presentation for the Archaeology Society. Project archaeologist Paul Williams was then left with the major task of piecing together the whole experience and writing a report for the Nova Scotia Museum.

Gains

Right: Two restored earthenware jugs, which were recovered from the Rockingham Inn site in pieces.

A major gain from the Rockingham Inn excavation was the mutually beneficial cooperation of so many interested organizations: The Nova Scotia Archaeology Society, Halifax District School Board, Halifax West High School, Rockingham Heritage Society, Saint Mary's University, Canadian Parks Service, Nova Scotia Museum, and other provincial government departments banded together to provide a valuable and engaging learning experience. The archaeology society pursued its mandate of promoting archaeology through young people, who will carry the mandate into the future. The Rockingham Heritage Society saw an historic building in their community re-emerge. For the students, the project was an extraordinary opportunity to study the history of their community in a way that could never be replicated in a classroom environment. For seventy-three teenagers (and their families), archaeology came alive in Halifax through community involvement in education.

Below: Hilary Beaumont and Michael Bawden, students at Armbrae Academy, recover artifacts in the Halifax Public Gardens after Hurricane Juan.

EXCAVATION EDUCATION "There's no better way to teach archaeology than doing it in the field," says Jonathan Fowler. "There are so many things you can't teach in the abstract."

In 1994, while studying anthropology at Saint Mary's University, Fowler participated in the Rockingham Inn project, serving as mentor to the high school students involved. Today, he teaches history and economics at Armbrae Academy (a Halifax independent school), as well as archaeology and history at Saint Mary's. And since 2001, Fowler has led a field school at Grand-Pré National Historic Site, located in the Annapolis Valley. For four or five weeks each summer, a dozen Saint Mary's students under Fowler's supervision work on excavating and analyzing the remains of a pre-Deportation Acadian settlement destroyed by New England soldiers in 1755.

After Hurricane Juan hit Halifax in September 2003, Halifax Regional Municipality contracted Fowler to conduct the recovery of archaeological remains in the Halifax Public Gardens. Situated in the downtown, the seventeen-acre Victorian gardens suffered extensive damage in the storm, and the uprooted trees had revealed hundreds of nineteenth-century artifacts. The original Horticultural Gardens, established in 1841, had occupied only the southern half of the current Public Gardens. The northern half, a swampy area, had remained part of the Halifax Common, and had been used as a dump until about 1870. Attesting to this history, students from Armbrae uncovered an assortment of ceramics, bottle glass, and clay pipe bowls and stems, deposited there as refuse. –RP

A Day at the Beach
The Coote Cove Archaeology Project

Laird Niven, In Situ–Cultural Heritage Research Group

J. L. Illsley High School teacher Bill Fougere examines an artifact during the field school.

Previous page: Crystal Crescent Beach. Archaeology site BcCv-1 is visible as a small headland in the centre of the image.

COOTE COVE WAS ONCE a small but vibrant fishing community located on a large headland approximately thirty-five kilometres from Halifax. However, by the second half of the nineteenth century, the community was all but abandoned. The former village is now part of Crystal Crescent Beach Provincial Park, a popular hiking and sun-bathing destination, and nature has almost completely reclaimed the land. The dozens of people who walk by the vegetation-covered cellars every day have no idea of the mystery they are passing—obscured from view and fading from local memory, the history of Coote Cove was nearly lost to neglect.

This began to change in 1990, however, when Stephen Powell conducted an archaeological survey of the park on behalf of the Nova Scotia Department of Lands and Forests and discovered twenty-six archaeological cellar depressions. Several years later, Bill Fougere, a teacher with J. L. Illsley High School in Spryfield, recognized the potential of the site as an educational tool, specifically as an archaeological field school for high school students.

Fougere envisioned the Coote Cove Archaeology Project as a partnership among schools, business, government, and the community. The schools would provide the students, who would be taught the fundamentals of archaeological fieldwork while excavating a significant archaeological site. It was hoped that eventually the project would involve many other disciplines within the schools, including science, geography, technology, and media classes. Funding, for the most part, would come from the private sector, with Teleglobe Canada as the first sponsor. The government would benefit from the data gathered by the project, which would be invaluable for future development and interpretation within the park. The community would benefit from the enhanced understanding of their origins and history generated by the archaeology. Finally, the complete package would help advance the cause of archaeology in Nova Scotia by increasing public awareness, enabling citizens to experience the discipline first-hand and to learn more about archaeology and its potential for expanding what we know of Nova Scotia's past.

In 1997, I was hired by J. L. Illsley and Halifax West high schools to direct the first field school for the Coote Cove Archaeology Project, scheduled to begin in October of that year. Before the actual fieldwork could start, however, background research into the history of Coote Cove had to be conducted. This research revealed that the history of the area was much older and more fascinating than first assumed.

The History of Coote Cove

The story of Coote Cove actually begins more than a thousand years before the arrival of European settlers, during what is known as the Maritime Woodland Period (2500 to 500 years ago), when the Mi'kmaq used the area as part of their seasonal migration through the province. This migration moved from the interior to the coast in early spring, as soon as the ice began breaking up on the rivers and along the shores. At that time, the Mi'kmaq would have found fish, shellfish, birds, and sea and land mammals in abundance. Evidence of this occupation had been reported by archaeologist Stephen Davis at a small headland, now completely lost to erosion, on the main beach of Crystal Crescent Beach Provincial Park. Further evidence of this occupation would be uncovered during the field school in 1997.

The first European settlers at Coote Cove were Scottish Methodists who landed in 1794 from Barrington, Nova Scotia. The village eventually included twenty-seven houses built along the shoreline. A more or less exposed beach would have aided the landing of boats, and skids were also built for hauling boats out of the water before winter. In the second half of the nineteenth century, the nature of the fishing grounds changed, and the fishermen found it necessary to travel farther offshore, which required larger vessels. As a consequence, Coote Cove became a less desirable location, and many families began moving to other areas, such as Sambro, most dismantling their houses and taking them along. By 1865, twenty families were living there, but by 1907 only three buildings remained.

The removal of a house from its foundation creates the potential for a unique archaeological site: one where the foundation becomes an archaeological feature, while the main structure has a new life as a building at a different location. At Coote Cove, I was fortunate enough to get details of a standing structure at Sambro Creek belonging to the Longard family that had been moved from Coote Cove in 1866. Shown in photographs provided by Nancy (Longard) Hood, the house was a very plain, one-and-a-half-storey building with a single central chimney. The front door of the house was located in the centre of the south wall. Once inside, one would face the stairway leading upstairs, with doors to rooms on the left and right. The hearths and chimney were located in the centre of the house, behind the stairway, with hearths in both of the downstairs rooms. The

The removal of a house from its foundation creates the potential for a unique archaeological site.

cellar was accessed from the outside via a door. The basic layout of the house was in the hall-and-parlour style, with the east room being the kitchen and the west room the more formal parlour. This background information would prove invaluable to the field school, allowing for the comparison of excavated architectural features with a documented Coote Cove house.

The Field School

With the background research complete, the field school portion of the project began. The first project was a collaboration between grade 11 academic J. L. Illsley students, supervised by teacher Bill Fougere, and Halifax West students, supervised by teacher David Williamson. A total of thirty-three students worked on the project between October 8 and October 23, 1997.

The field school was divided into four basic sections: archaeological surveying; archaeological excavation; artifact analysis and interpretation; and the final report. (A fifth component, background research, had been completed prior to the start of the field school. It would usually be the first component completed.)

THE DIGITAL AGE IN ARCHAEOLOGY With the advent of the digital age, archaeology has moved out of the ground and into space. Where once an archaeological site was meticulously documented on paper using a ruler and pencil, it is now more precisely plotted using satellite-aided Geographical Positioning System technology. Artifacts and site features are mapped to the millimetre using the optical surveying instrument known as the total station, and the results are plotted in three dimensions with computer-aided drafting software. Additionally, site photographs are now taken with high-resolution digital cameras.

Once the excavation is completed, all of this digital information is then brought together using Geographical Information System software, which can then be used for advanced analysis, interpretation, and presentation. The ability to reconstruct a site using this digital technology is unprecedented, and it offers archaeologists insights into the past that were unthinkable a generation ago. And now, thanks to the internet, the results of even the smallest excavation can be easily shared with the world.–LN

The archaeological survey is the most basic means of site identification employed by archaeologists, and it is usually designed based on data uncovered during the initial background research. In this case, a map supplied by Nancy Hood—which had been made by her mother, Evelyn Longard, in 1960—showed the locations of all of the former houses in Coote Cove as well as the names of the occupants. This map had been used by Stephen Powell during his 1990 survey, and he succeeded in identifying where each of the houses depicted once stood, by means of the archaeological cellar depressions. While it was not strictly necessary, therefore, for the field school to survey the entire site again, the Longard map and Powell's findings served as useful guideposts, as the students were introduced to the basic concepts of archaeological surveying.

While site surveying is an essential but low profile part of any archaeology project, excavation is the most prominent component—and consequently, the one with which most members of the public are familiar. Once a location has been chosen for excava-

Opposite page: Evelyn Longard created this map of Coote Cove in 1960. The 1997 excavation took place at the location marked "Operation 1."

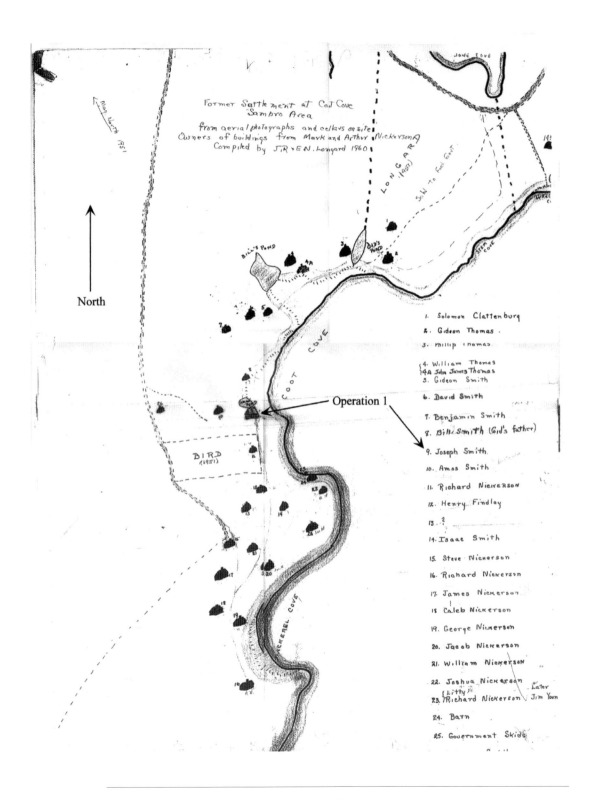

Former Settlement at Coot Cove
Sambro Area

from aerial photographs and cellars on site
Owners of buildings from Mark and Arthur Nickerson
Compiled by J.R. & E.N. Longard 1960

North

1. Solomon Clattenburg
2. Gideon Thomas
3. Phillip Thomas
4. William Thomas
4A. John James Thomas
5. Gideon Smith
6. David Smith
7. Benjamin Smith
8. Bill Smith (Gid's father)
9. Joseph Smith
10. Amos Smith
11. Richard Nickerson
12. Henry Findlay
13. ?
14. Isaac Smith
15. Steve Nickerson
16. Richard Nickerson
17. James Nickerson
18. Caleb Nickerson
19. George Nickerson
20. Jacob Nickerson
21. William Nickerson
22. Joshua Nickerson (Litty)   Later
23. Richard Nickerson   Jim Yoon
24. Barn
25. Government Skids

Operation 1

tion, a physical grid is laid over the site, which is essential for maintaining both horizontal and vertical control. Each artifact, feature, and soil lot is recorded within this grid, allowing for the reconstruction of the site on computer during the analysis phase.

The essential excavation tool of the archaeologist is the mason's trowel, used to scrape soil from the unit in a very controlled manner. The loose soil is emptied from a dust pan into a bucket, and then sifted using a fine screen to search for smaller artifacts that may have been overlooked. Any artifacts uncovered by the troweling are left in place until they can be recorded. Once measurement is complete, the artifact is removed and placed into a marked bag. Attention is also paid to major changes in soil colour or type, which are usually an indication of different events; the soil accumulated during the occupation of a house, for example, will be a different colour than undisturbed natural soil.

Excavating Joseph Smith's House

Excavation units in 1997. The sub-operations (sub-ops) were designed to recover data about the house of Joseph Smith.

With these excavation concepts in hand, the students were ready to dig. The primary objective of the 1997 Coote Cove Archaeology Project was to examine one site, officially designated BcCv-1 and identified on the Longard map as being the former house of Joseph Smith, one of the founders of Coote Cove. The site was chosen for its proximity to the parking area, making the movement of equipment easier. Furthermore, its prominent position near the walking paths gave the field school greater exposure to the public, as heightened community awareness of archaeology was one of the project's goals. The research objective was to answer some basic questions about the site: Was this a building and, if so, what function did it serve? When was the building occupied? What did the building look like?

BcCv-1 is located on a small point above the second Crystal Crescent beach, in a well-travelled area with paths creating a triangular border around the site. The setting is one not only of great beauty but also of practical function—direct access to the beach and the nearby cove would have been desirable features to the fishermen who settled the area. When the students set to work, the area was covered in low vegetation, which obscured many of the features on the ground. The feature chosen for excavation was interpreted as being the main cellar depression, measuring 4.5 metres square by 1.5 metres deep. Once the brush was cleared, however, the stone outline of the west half of the house was revealed. This new element was 6.5 x 5.5 metres, a more respectable size for a house. A square formation of rocks was uncovered outside of the south wall, and this was interpreted as a porch. During the clearing, a wall was also revealed twelve metres to the northwest, and a stone well was found thirty-four metres to the northwest.

Four excavation units were placed over the area, which was designed to reveal data about the architecture of the building, as well as recover artifacts that might provide an occupation date for the site. The first excavation unit (sub-operation A) was one metre by six metres and began outside the west wall, extending east into the west half of the structure. The second (sub-operation B) was a one-by-eight-metre unit placed on the edge of the east side of the depression, running north to south. The third (sub-operation C) was a one-by-two-metre unit placed eight metres east of the cellar depression (the purpose of this unit was to examine the possibility that there were intact First Nations features on the site, but the results were negative). Finally, the last unit (sub-operation D) measured one metre by six metres and ran west from the south end of sub-operation B through the cellar depression. The physical grid laid over these excavation units divided them into square metre sections, each of which was worked on by three or four students.

The excavation revealed that the building had been made up of two sections and measured approximately 11.0 x 4.5 metres. The eastern half of the structure was dominated by a 4.5-metre square depression, which was 1.5 metres deep; the western half was delineated by a rough stone foundation measuring 5.5 metres square. Excavation did not reveal the relationship between the halves of the building—whether, for

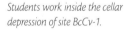

Students work inside the cellar depression of site BcCv-1.

instance, there was a wall between them. While the north, south, and west sides of the structure were well defined, the east edge of the depression was much less distinct.

The excavation in sub-operation A uncovered many rocks, some quite large, that appeared to form a level line running west to east, and up to the end of the unit. This feature may have been a pier or footing on which wooden sleepers were laid and into which floor joists were placed. Such construction would have compensated for the site's slight slope to the west. Meanwhile, excavation at the east end of sub-operation A found a quantity of brick rubble, including a yellow fire brick, confirming the location of one fireplace. Finally, a concentration of rocks at the south end of sub-operation B was interpreted as the remains of an external entrance to the cellar.

The most interesting architectural aspect of the excavation was being able to compare the features the field school uncovered at BcCv-1 with the known floor plan of the Longard house, which had been relocated from Coote Cove to Sambro Creek in 1866. All of the features from BcCv-1 are reflected in the Sambro Creek house. Entrance into the house would have been through a small porch, after which there were rooms to the right and the left. The cellar depression and the uncovered artifacts suggest that the room to the right was the kitchen. The room to the left was the parlour, and there was a fireplace in each room. Therefore, of the four research questions asked above, three were answered from the excavation. This structure was indeed a building, more specifically a house, and it was built in the hall-and-parlour style. The question of the occupation date of Joseph Smith's home would be revealed during the artifact analysis.

Here the Longard plan of Joseph Smith's house (l) is compared to excavated features of site BcCv-1.

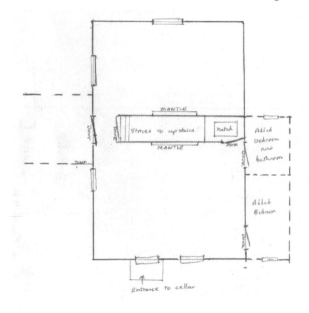

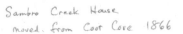

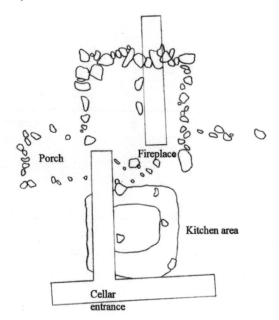

Artifact Analysis and Interpretation

During excavation, one person's trash becomes the archaeologist's treasure. The discarded garbage of a family can give insights into occupation date and social status, among other things. The 1997 Coote Cove Archaeology Project uncovered 3,600 artifacts, nearly half of which were Mi'kmaq and dated to the Maritime Woodland Period. While the vast majority of these artifacts were stone flakes, also found were two arrowheads, hide scrapers, some pottery, and a quahog shell that appears to have been used as a shaper or smoother. All of the First Nations artifacts were recovered from disturbed contexts, the original site most likely destroyed during the digging of the cellar.

Ceramics are generally the most useful artifacts for establishing an occupation date on eighteenth- and nineteenth-century sites. The majority of the ceramics from BcCv-1 were kitchen-related—plates, bowls, cups, jugs, etc.—manufactured in Great Britain or North America and dating to the middle of the nineteenth century. There were very few fragments of "wine" bottles recovered. This was not surprising as the residents of the house were strict Methodists and would have completely abstained from alcohol. While they may not have been drinkers, they seemed to have enjoyed smoking, as a minimum of nine different clay tobacco pipes were recovered.

While the ceramics suggest a broad date spanning the nineteenth century, two artifacts provided much more specific dates. The first was a button with an Irish harp surrounded by shamrocks stamped on its face. Around the harp were the words "Repeal of the Union God Save the Queen." These few words have great political significance. The saying was the rallying cry of Daniel O'Connell, the Catholic "Liberator" of Ireland who led a campaign for the repeal of the union with Great Britain from 1840 to 1847. The timeframe suggested by this artifact fits in very well with the known circumstances of the site's occupation, and gives insight into the public sympathy the people of Halifax may have had for the Irish cause. The second diagnostic artifact was a Nova Scotia halfpenny token dated 1856.

The Final Report

The 1997 field school at Coote Cove was a great success and served to raise the profile of archaeology in the province. The students synthesized the gathered data into an enjoyable, multi-media presentation for the public and the press, held at J. L. Illsley High School. The Coote Cove Archaeology Project continued until 2001, with a new site started in 1999, but changes to the Nova Scotia history curriculum meant that archaeology did not fit in the same way, and the project was cancelled.

Steamship China from Halifax Harbour

Greg Cochkanoff, Atlantic Catch Data Limited

WHEN Bob Chaulk, Dana Sheppard, and I made our first dives into Halifax Harbour, it was because of a general curiosity about what was in the dark waters of the historic harbour. Halifax has been an incredibly important port since the first explorations of the New World, and we expected to discover a wealth of artifacts as we tentatively entered the harbour from shore.

Above: An artifact of the pad-dlesteamer Pacific. *The* Pacific *was launched in 1854 for the Sydney & Melbourne Steam Packet Company.*

Right: Diver Bob Chaulk in the split rock, a large erratic, or glacial boulder, cleanly cracked in two at the bottom of the Narrows. The abundant and healthy marine life and hard, gravelly bottom are due to constant ocean currents. This photograph was taken using natural light at a depth of 9.8 metres.

Opposite page: Diver Bob Chaulk emerges from a rewarding dive along the Halifax waterfront, holding a butter pat with the logo of the Red Cross Line.

Diving in the Harbour

That first dive took place on April 18, 1982. At the bottom of a steep underwater slope, which began just off the shore, was the flat bottom of the shipping channel, about twenty-three metres deep. The marine environment was surprisingly healthy and natural—the strong tidal currents brought clean, clear water from the open ocean, sweeping away the silt and sediments and leaving a hard, gravelly bottom. Marine life was abundant, thriving in the constant currents. Colourful anemones by the thousands festooned the rocks, while crabs, starfish, and other bottom dwellers crawled about everywhere. It was a relief to discover that much of the deepwater portions of Halifax Harbour were largely unaffected by the pollution frequently seen along the wharves of the Halifax waterfront.

That first, cursory exploration only piqued our interest in the harbour, and countless subsequent dives took place. Chaulk, Sheppard, and I used compasses for navigation, relying on erratics (large boulders dropped by the glaciers) and rock-filled cribs (which once held footings for a railway bridge that spanned the Narrows in the late nineteenth century) as landmarks.

Almost any area of the harbour was accessible if we took advantage of the clear ocean waters that flood with the tide into the harbour twice a day. It quickly became clear that diving is best done in the dead of winter, when runoff is at its lowest and there are few pleasure craft to contend with. By coordinating dives with Halifax Harbour traffic control authorities and issuing official "notices to mariners," the hazards of encountering huge ocean-going container ships and other harbour traffic were minimized.

Over time, we pried open the door to what could be described as the largest, most complex archaeological site in Nova Scotia: the bottom of Halifax Harbour.

The Steamship China Catalogue

Our initial suspicions were gradually confirmed: scattered all over the harbour seabed were artifacts lost and discarded from passing ships, and the detritus of the human occupation of Halifax since its earliest days. Every dive was filled with new discoveries. Bottles, cameras, clay pipes, vending machines, ships' fittings, bowling balls, navigation instruments, guns, money, bombs, swords, art objects, false teeth, crock jugs, pocket watches, church crosses, airplane wrecks, and shipwrecks were all found in the harbour. Scattered among all these objects were thousands of fragments of china: broken cups, saucers, dinner plates, milk pitchers, serving platters, egg cups, butter pats, bedpans, pickle dishes, serving bowls, and more.

Prop wash blasted through several feet of seabed debris. These holes can be filled in and new ones created as different ships manoeuvre around Halifax harbour. Dozens of fragments of china, and one or two intact dishes, can be seem amongst the debris of a newly-blasted seabed crater.

Many of these china fragments bore the crests and names of shipping companies. From the earliest days of ocean travel, proud ship owners have decorated their shipboard china with their company names, emblems, and house flags; for just as long, crews have been tossing their garbage, including this china, overboard. Now these durable pieces of china lie scattered throughout the harbour as reminders of the thousands of ships that have visited the port of Halifax over more than two hundred years.

It became clear to me that these china patterns should be collected and catalogued, and so I started the steamship china catalogue (a systematized list with descriptions), which has been steadily growing ever since. For each pattern, I record as much detail as possible: where the china was found, in what quantity, and, most importantly, which company it represents. Then the company is researched—its years of operation, the ships it owned, the ports it serviced, and its reasons for being in Halifax.

Well-known companies such as the Cunard and White Star lines are easy to research, because these companies were frequent visitors to Halifax, and their histories

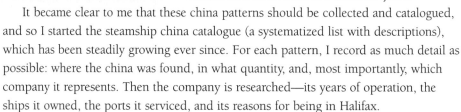

SAMUEL CUNARD Samuel Cunard (1787–1865) of Halifax became a major player in transatlantic communications between North America and Britain when he developed a scheduled steamship service between the two continents. The "Cunarders," as the steamships were known, transported both passengers and coveted news of European happenings. By the early 1800s, Cunard easily held his own with American and European tycoons, with fleets of successful, fast vessels, and profitable contacts in exotic trading hubs such as the West Indies. China on board Cunard's first steamships of the 1840s carried the same logo as those visiting today: a lion holding a globe. –SM

Diver Bob Chaulk floats beside one of the propellers on a harbour tugboat. Without rudders, these vessels can swivel their two propellers in any direction. When their propwash hits a solid wharf, or the side of an enormous oceangoing ship, the flow can be directed down to the seabed, scouring craters in the sediments and scattering artifacts.

have been well documented. Dozens of other examples have proven more difficult to identify. Researching these obscure and little-known companies provides a glimpse into the development of the transatlantic steamship, as well as the importance of Halifax as an international seaport.

Some of the china patterns found represent companies run by entrepreneurs who pioneered new technologies and designs in steamships. A few patterns are from companies that probably operated only one ship before failing and disappearing into the recesses of history, defeated by changing technologies, poor business decisions, or just plain bad luck. As short-lived failures, these companies left few reminders of their existence, and there are scant references to them in the popular histories of ocean travel. A broken piece of china can be valuable physical evidence of these companies' presence in Halifax.

One such ship is the *Pacific*, launched in 1854 for the Sydney & Melbourne Steam Packet Company. It was designed to be a fast and economical ship, incorporating all the latest technologies. One of the first large steamers built with an iron hull, it helped usher in a new generation of ocean travel. Its hull was built on the "wave form" design, which meant that its sides ran parallel for just under a metre, at midships. Although these features were novel, its 8.2-metre-wide paddle wheels were technologically outmoded; the newly developed screw propeller was proving much more efficient. The *Pacific* completed four transatlantic crossings for the Galway Line before being sold. Its new owners replaced its paddle wheels with a propeller, yet it was unable to keep up

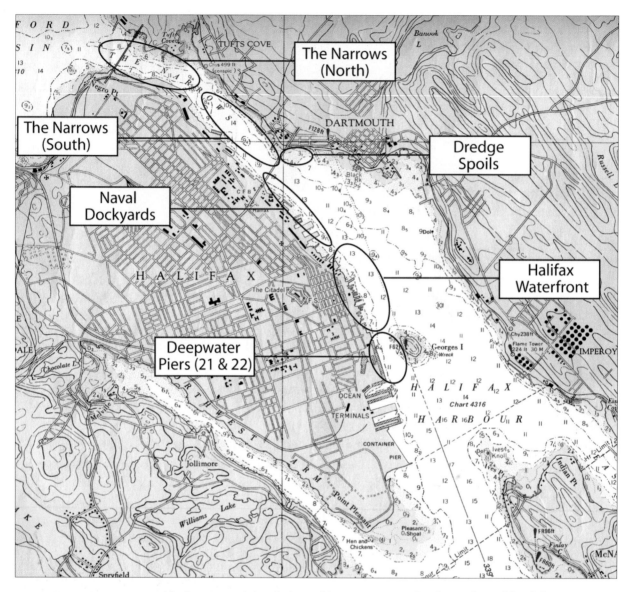

The Narrows
(North)

The Narrows
(South)

Dredge
Spoils

Naval
Dockyards

Halifax
Waterfront

Deepwater
Piers (21 & 22)

Portion of Nautical Chart #4385, "Osborne Head to Betty Island." The chart shows areas where concentrations of steamship china may be found, although isolated finds have been made throughout the entire harbour, its approaches, and the Northwest Arm.

with the ever-evolving designs of its competitors. Condemned to a life of obscurity, it was largely forgotten and eventually wrecked off the Shetland Islands. Today, references to the *Pacific's* unique place in the development of transatlantic steamers are rare, because the ship was a technological hybrid that failed. Still, concrete proof of the ship's presence in Halifax Harbour is noteworthy to those interested in the history of steam travel.

Other china patterns found in the harbour, especially those with complicated names resulting from amalgamations, give a glimpse into the high-stakes world of steam travel—mergers, buyouts, massive failures, massive successes. The capital-intensive business of building and operating ocean-going steamships provided for some unusual business relationships, further confused by the effects of war and government involvement.

Over the years, various groups of sport divers have undertaken the challenge of exploring the seabed between Halifax and Dartmouth. Upon learning of the steamship china collection, many in the sport diving community began to collect samples for the catalogue. And so, through the ongoing efforts of sport divers such as Thierry Papion, Jason Kennedy, and more than a dozen others, the project has continued to grow.

Diving at the Naval Dockyards

In 1999, with what was now an intimate knowledge of much of the bottom of Halifax Harbour, and with hundreds of steamship china patterns documented, Bob Chaulk, Dana Sheppard, and I soon turned our attentions to the holy grail of diving in the harbour: the naval dockyards. The Navy expanded their Halifax dockyards just before World War One by appropriating the deepwater wharves used by all the transatlantic steamship companies. During the nineteenth century all the major companies—Cunard, White Star, Norddeutscher Lloyd Breman, and dozens of others—berthed at the jetties where destroyers and submarines are located today. We hoped that diving around the naval jetties would yield abundant examples of pre-twentieth-century steamship china from companies active during the heyday of steamship development.

It took a month for the commanding officers of the Halifax Naval Dockyards to grant the small diving group unrestricted access to the entire naval dockyards. This, the area where Samuel Cunard once berthed his first steamships, should have been an immense treasure trove that cast new light on Halifax's seafaring history. But unfortunately, dredging, new construction, and landfills have totally obliterated all evidence of this most historic piece of Halifax's waterfront. After several dives and careful searching, one solitary piece of steamship china (from the Royal Mail Steam Packet Company) that predated the naval dockyards was discovered—hardly the anticipated bonanza of artifacts. Everything was out of reach, buried under millions of tons of rock, concrete, and landfill.

The forays into the naval dockyards were not entirely without reward, however. Subsequent dives took place in Navy-controlled sections (previously off-limits) of the deepwater channel, and these efforts uncovered numerous examples of naval china that spoke to the importance of Halifax as a naval port.

Royal Navy and Royal Canadian Navy ships at HMC Dockyard, October 16, 1942

STEAMSHIP CHINA RECOVERED FROM HALIFAX HARBOUR Left, a creamer from the Newfoundland Coastal S.S. Company displays one of several patterns originating from local coastal services that plied the waters of Atlantic Canada. Centre, a serving bowl is emblazoned with the logo of the Mississippi & Dominion Steam Ship Company, one of the many incarnations of what eventually became the White Star Dominion Line. Right, a cup and saucer from the Quebec Steamship Company. The cup is composed of two fragments recovered months apart. The matching saucer was recovered in the same area on yet another dive. –GC

A SPOON AND FORK FROM THE RED CROSS LINE This spoon and fork belonged to the SS *Stephano* and SS *Florizel*, both ships of the Red Cross Line. The ships were intimately involved with the seal hunt and other maritime activities in the waters off Nova Scotia and Newfoundland. They both met tragic ends, the *Stephano* torpedoed in 1916 and the *Florizel* wrecked in 1918. –GC

CURIOUS HAND ETCHINGS have been documented on dozens of fragments of Royal Navy china. Most of the etchings comprise Roman numerals, yet many do not follow the conventional Roman numeral system. Other etchings comprise simple geometric symbols and markings, perhaps for personal identification. Prior to 1907, sailors were responsible for providing their own dishes, as the Royal Navy did not provide shipboard china for use by the crew. These two bowl fragments each have such etchings on the bottom rims; one still has a large barnacle attached. –GC

Hundreds, even thousands, of examples of Royal Navy and other military china were found scattered on the sea floor. (In some areas of the deepwater channels, Royal Navy china is significantly more abundant than any other types of china. This is to be expected, since, for many decades, Halifax was one of the Royal Navy's primary North American bases.) Steeped in tradition and ceremony, much of the Royal Navy china is highly ornate. Oversized images of the Crown and proud images of warships and flags are common, with a few examples referring to specific ships. The sheer volume of naval china required that a separate catalogue be established to handle this growing collection.

Disappearing Stories

Each individual piece of china has a unique story to tell. Collectively, these sherds speak volumes about the importance of Halifax as a commercial port and naval base. Unfortunately, the bottom of Halifax Harbour is a very unstable environment. New construction, infilling, dredging, and constant ship movements make the sea floor a dynamic place, and every artifact in Halifax Harbour is under constant risk of having an

Diver Dana Sheppard stands over dozens of dishes and bowls recovered during one of the team's first dives in the Naval Dockyards. The team's initial excitement was tempered when they discovered that most of this material originated from World War Two to modern day.

anchor weighing several tonnes dropped on it. Recently, a jack-up drill rig's legs penetrated 4.6 metres into the midst of one of the most historic anchorages in Halifax Harbour. It is impossible to know what important artifacts may have been destroyed.

Today, the steamship china project continues, with sport divers continuing to submit examples to be catalogued. However, the project is a race against time. Firstly, plans drafted for continued expansion of port facilities in Halifax have sparked more

CHINA PATTERNS OF THE ALLAN LINE, perhaps Canada's premier shipping company of the nineteenth century. It is represented by more than ten china patterns. The original name, "Montreal Ocean Steamship Company," registered by the Allan brothers in 1854, was later changed to the Allan Line to reflect the name in common usage. This company operated both steam ships and sailing ships, but the red pennant was flown above the tricolour "house" flag only on steamers. The same distinction applies to the house flag depicted on shipboard china, as seen in one of these examples. Allan Line steamers visited Halifax regularly for more than fifty years until taken over in 1917 by Canadian Pacific. –GC dredging and infilling. Secondly, terrorist alerts following the tragic events of September 11, 2001, have prompted authorities to place tighter restrictions on diving in Halifax Harbour, making it increasingly difficult to visit particularly rich deposits, like those that may be found around Piers 21 and 22. And finally, ships of massive proportions are now visiting these wharves. In 2004, for instance, Cunard Line's *Queen Mary 2*—the largest cruise liner afloat—visited Halifax twice. Its novel thrusters, extending below its keel, have eliminated the need for tugboats to help it dock, despite its enormous size— but these thrusters create new disturbances on the seabed, causing fragments of historic china to swirl like leaves in a whirlwind as the ship manoeuvres around our historic wharves. Who knows? Perhaps a diver a hundred years from now will be delighted to come across the *QM2*'s china on the harbour bottom.

ROYAL NAVY CHINA Many examples of Royal Navy china spanning many decades and in a variety of patterns and mess numbers have been documented. Some examples identify specific ships, such as the bowl with the solid blue rim, which bears the name H.M.S. *Northampton*. –GC

Divers Bob Chaulk and Dana Sheppard monitor a container ship and tugboat about to pass under the A. Murray MacKay bridge. Once the vessels have passed, the divers will continue their exploration of the deepwater channel. This type of diving requires a spirit of adventure. Divers must avoid many potential hazards by exercising caution and following safety procedures developed over hundreds of dives.

The steamship china catalogue project, conducted entirely by volunteer sport divers working under government permit and the guidance of professional archaeologists, is an example of useful co-operation among various groups. Today, hundreds of examples of china have been documented, and copies of the china catalogue have been turned over to the Nova Scotia government, without taxpayer expense or disruption of commercial and industrial activity within Halifax Harbour. The project continues, as small groups of dedicated individuals venture into the poorly explored aquatic wilderness between Halifax and Dartmouth. The next time you cross one of the harbour bridges, you might want to see if you can spot their bubbles.

The Marine Archaeology of Halifax Harbour

Gordon Fader, Geological Survey of Canada (Atlantic)
Bedford Institute of Oceanography

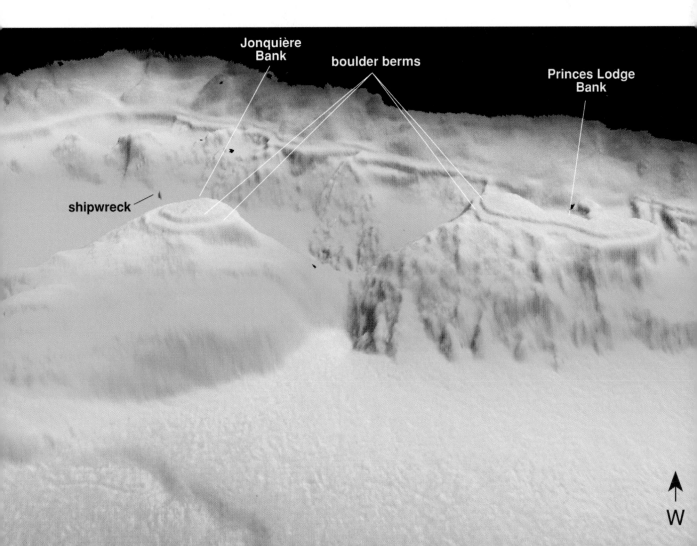

Jonquière Bank

boulder berms

Princes Lodge Bank

shipwreck

W

H ALIFAX HARBOUR IS A SIGNIFICANT REPOSITORY for many submerged cultural heritage resources. For as long as the region has been a site of human occupation—since the final retreat of glaciers about twelve thousand years ago—the harbour has collected the traces of human activity. Unlike adjacent land areas where the terrain has been severely altered through deforestation and construction, much of the seabed represents a cumulative history of activities, which can be understood using an array of modern seabed mapping and surveying technologies. It is a common misconception that marine archaeology is confined to the discovery and exploration of shipwrecks. In addition to the vessels and artifacts that might be recovered, the study of the seabed itself is vital to understanding our maritime past.

Mapping and Surveying the Harbour

In the late 1980s, the Geological Survey of Canada at the Bedford Institute of Oceanography shifted its research from studies offshore on the continental shelf to the bays and estuaries along the coastline. Halifax Harbour was one of the first near-shore areas to be systematically studied with a suite of new and improved seabed mapping systems. It was also one of the first areas in the world to be surveyed with "multibeam bathymetric sonar mapping systems." Multibeam bathymetry uses sound waves to sweep the seabed, providing complete images of topography with very high resolution. The imagery produced is as though the water were drained from the ocean and the seabed was viewed from an airplane, with the surface shaded by a setting sun. This technology has provided for an unprecedented characterization of the floor of Halifax Harbour and led to the new understanding of how the harbour has been shaped by erosion, currents, and sediment deposition. A variety of mapping systems was used in addition to the multibeam bathymetry, including sidescan sonars, seismic reflection systems, seabed grab samplers, corers, video, photography, and observations from submersibles and remotely operated vehicles (ROVs). Based on this work, which spanned fifteen years, it can be said that the anthropogenic (human) imprint on the harbour bottom is overwhelming. It is so pervasive that it becomes difficult at times to avoid all the bottom debris to sample the natural seabed.

The first two harbour features investigated during the study were associated with popular, long-standing local myths. One of these was the existence of a secret tunnel running underneath the harbour floor, connecting Citadel Hill with Georges Island. (While it may seem unlikely that such an engineering feat could have been accomplished in the nineteenth century in secret, four previously unknown tunnels were discovered beneath Halifax streets over the past eighty years, evidently linking the Citadel with the waterfront in case of invasion). The other legend concerned a crater on the harbour floor, supposedly formed by the blast of the 1917 Halifax Explosion (caused by the

Opposite page: The July 18, 1989 Chronicle-Herald *reports the discovery of the remains of the first two Halifax Harbour bridges by Gordon Fader and Robert Miller.*

Previous page: A three-dimensional multibeam bathymetric image of the western side of Bedford Basin, taken from the east. The boulder berms clearly show as ridges near the present shoreline (black to orange transition) and define the location of former islands known as Jonquière Bank and the proposed Princes Lodge Bank. There is an unidentified shipwreck to the west of Jonquière Bank.

Gordon Fader, left, and Robert Miller, geologists at the Bedford Institute of Oceanography, study maps locating two bridges which once spanned Halifax harbour. The scientists found remnants of the hundred-year-old bridges while conducting a geological survey.

Wamboldt-Waterfield/Darrin Colp

Remnants of harbour bridges found

Scientists discount curse as cause of collapses

Three times a bridge o'er these waves shall rise
Built by the paleface, so strong and wise
Three times shall fall like a dying breath
In storm and silence and last in death.

— old Micmac curse

By JANICE TIBBETTS
Dartmouth Bureau

The first two Halifax-Dartmouth bridges — one which collapsed in a hurricane and the second which washed away on a quiet night nearly 100 years ago — have been found resting in their watery grave 500 metres south of the A. Murray MacKay bridge.

Robert Miller and Gordon Fader, geologists with Energy, Mines and Resources' Atlantic Geoscience Centre at the Bedford Institute of Oceanography, stumbled upon the remnants of the bridges while completing a geological survey of Halifax harbour last month for the harbour clean-up project.

The survey, which was the first to be done in the harbour, also unveiled several shipwrecks and a sunken aircraft.

Remnants of the two bridges were found stretching across The Narrows, the narrowest section of the harbour, 17-20 metres below the surface. They were built in 1884-85 and 1892. When they stood, the bridges reached from the current Volvo plant pier in Halifax to Norris Cove in Dartmouth.

See BRIDGES page 20

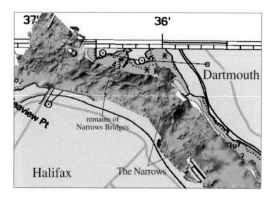

Colour-coded multibeam bathymetric map of the seabed of the Narrows. The map shows the shape of the seabed and the remains of the first two bridges as a linear pile of debris. Water depths range up to twenty-three metres.

collision of the French munitions ship the *Mont Blanc*, which was carrying over two million kilos of explosives, with the Belgian relief vessel, the *Imo*). While the investigation of the harbour seabed revealed that neither the story of the crater nor of the tunnel had any substance, the seabed features which were uncovered offered rare insight into a submerged part of Halifax's history. Three especially interesting features revealed by the harbour mapping project are: the original bridges of the Narrows, the former lowered shorelines and islands of Bedford Basin, and the *Havana* and *Gertrude de Costa* shipwrecks in the inner harbour.

First Narrows Bridges

On November 10, 1989, while surveying the seabed of the Narrows of the harbour aboard the CCGS *Navicula*, geological technician Bob Miller and I (a marine geologist) discovered an unusual pattern of large rectangular objects spanning the Narrows from Norris Cove to Pier 9. Like most Haligonians, we had no recollection of former construction activities in the Narrows, but archival research soon revealed that we had found the remains of not one, but two original harbour-crossing bridges. News of the discovery quickly spread and, within the next few days, became a Canadian national media event.

Subsequent investigations with cameras, samplers, and other acoustic systems revealed not only details of the bridges' remains but, more importantly, the story of why both bridges collapsed. The two bridges were built at the same location, approximately five hundred metres south of the present A. Murray MacKay Bridge. The first bridge was completed in May 1884, constructed of pine and hemlock from areas of Cumberland County, and steel from Londonderry and New Glasgow. It contained a steel swing section made by the Starr Manufacturing Company of Dartmouth that was positioned near the Dartmouth shoreline and designed to allow ships to move into Bedford Basin. It was curved toward the basin to protect it from spring ice floes. The bridge had been built on piers with each base containing twenty tonnes of rock ballast. Almost half a kilometre long, it was built mainly as a railway bridge, but also featured a foot path alongside the track. An average of 125 train cars used the bridge daily.

On September 7, 1891, a hurricane descended on Halifax Harbour, with winds reportedly as high as 110 kilometres per hour. Much damage was done to the docks of the harbour, and the bridge collapsed during the night. It was then believed that the curved section had caught the wind that came from the east, and nearly the entire structure washed away. All that remained were a few broken timbers and some trestles in shallow water.

The first Harbour bridge. The swing section opens in the background near the Dartmouth side.

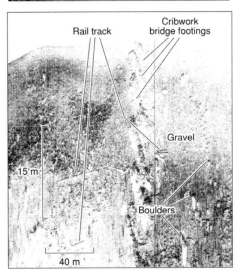

A sidescan sonar record of the seabed of the Narrows, showing details of the bridge remains. The bridge footings consist of boulder-filled cribwork, and rail track is scattered across the seabed.

After much debate, a second bridge was built in the same location using piles thrust into the Narrows seabed. As the bridge appeared unstable after completion, granite blocks were placed on the harbour floor beside the bridge and connected with torqued cables. Despite these efforts, the second bridge floated away on July 6, 1893, after a strong tide essentially lifted it from its foundation on a quiet summer night.

Surveying the Narrows revealed that much of the original cribwork of the first bridge is still intact, rising above the bottom of the harbour by several metres. Both twisted and straight sections of rail track remain on the seabed alongside the huge granite blocks used to anchor the second bridge. The cribwork, footings, and track are covered with a dense marine growth of sea anemones and other benthic (or seabed dwelling) species fed by the nutrient-rich, fast-moving waters of the Narrows. Here, the harbour floor consists of gravel and boulders, and is swept clean of muddy sediments by strong tidal currents. This combination of geological and oceanographic conditions were unfavourable for the type of bridge construction used. The high energy of the hurricane that brought down the original bridge separated it from its cribwork base. The second disaster was likely the result of the pilings failing to property penetrate the hard seabed of the Narrows, so this bridge was never properly founded. It is comforting to know that the A. Murray MacKay Bridge (which opened to traffic in 1970), though built in the same area, is founded on solid bedrock.

The remains of the first two bridges lie as prominent features of the Narrows. A large amount of debris, including rail track, wire, bottles, and material possibly discarded or lost during construction of the bridges, litters the adjacent seabed. In the future, dredging and removal of the old bridge footings may be required for safe passage of post-Panamex, deep-draught container ships, as the container facility in Bedford Basin is expanded. Before such an excavation could take place, there will need to be a proper archaeological investigation of the bridge remains, construction techniques, and associated artifacts.

Lake Bedford and the Islands

The survey of Halifax Harbour offered crucial insight into the history of sea level change in the area. Understanding sea level change has great archeological value: the shorelines where early peoples once congregated are now submerged, and so are the artifacts they left behind. The multibeam bathymetric mapping of the harbour, combined with analysis of cores and seabed samples, uncovered the evidence of thousands of years of post-glacial landscape and seabedscape development.

When the last glaciers receded from the region, approximately twelve thousand years ago, much of the area of Halifax Harbour was occupied by a series of ten or so lakes, connected by an early ancestral Sackville River system. The former marine shore-

MULTIBEAM BATHYMETRY Before the advent of multibeam bathymetric seabed mapping, scientists and hydrographers learned about the depths of the ocean and the shape of the seabed through the use of echosounders. These systems operated by sending out from the ship a single sound pulse that bounced off the seabed, and the time it took for the signal to return was converted to water depth. Since survey lines were never close together, only part of the seabed was accurately mapped with this method.

Multibeam bathymetry relies on the integration of four technologies: powerful computer processors, accurate positioning systems (Global Positioning Satellites), precise motion detectors on ships to measure rolling and pitching, and multibeam transducers that produce multiple acoustic signals in a fan-shaped pattern to cover large areas of the seabed.

During the past decade, multibeam bathymetric mapping has further developed so that the systems can now define not only water depth but also the material at the seabed, such as bedrock, sand, and mud. Visualization software allows virtual fly-throughs across the seabed, as if the water were drained away and the viewer were travelling in a plane. Offering exceptional resolution, multibeam bathymetry has allowed marine geologists and archaeologists to study the seabed as never before. –GF

line of 11,600 years ago has been clearly identified at a location about twenty kilometres off Chebucto Head, at a depth of sixty-five to seventy metres. The area of Bedford Basin, meanwhile, was occupied by at least three connected lakes: one in Bedford Bay, one in the Basin proper, and another in Fairview Cove. The water level in these lakes was defined by the discovery of former shorelines in the basin at a present depth of twenty-three metres. Two continuous berms (ridges) composed of boulders ring the basin at this depth, and would have been formed by seasonal freezing and ice expansion of the lakes' waters. (Similar ridges are common features today around the shores of many Nova Scotian lakes.)

A colour-coded multibeam bathymetric map of the seabed of Bedford Basin. Water depths here range up to seventy-one metres. Boulder berms representing a former shoreline occur at a depth of twenty-three metres and ring most of the Basin, defining islands that existed mainly on the western side.

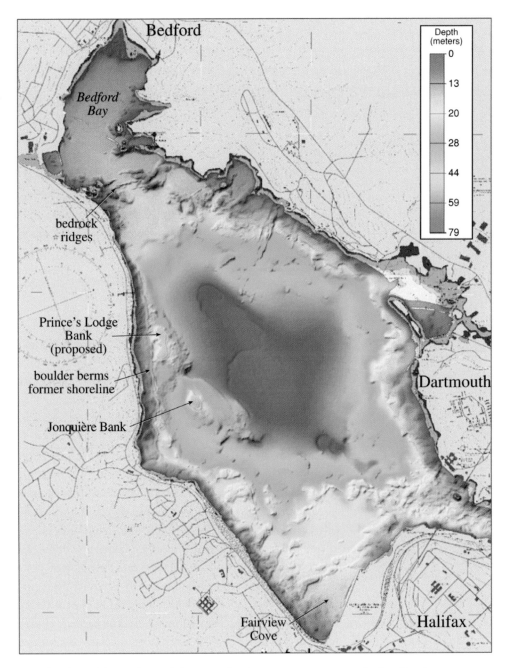

Clearly visible on the multibeam and sidescan sonar imagery, the boulder berms were further investigated with ROV cameras. The berms separate two distinct types of terrain. Above the former shoreline marked by the berms, the seabed is flattened and smoother, and is largely gravel covered with little mud. This is the result of a process called marine transgression, whereby the seabed above the berms passed through the

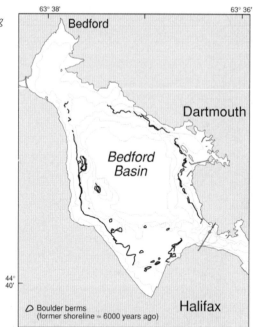

A map of Bedford Basin showing the interpreted location of the former shoreline and many islands, which existed between 12,000 and 5,800 years ago.

beach zone of the rising sea when the former lake (Lake Bedford) was converted to a marine bay with the return of sea level from its glacial low stand. The timing of this dramatic change from lake to ocean is well constrained by analyses and dating of organisms that lived in the sediments; the process happened 5,800 years ago. Prior to this time, Bedford Basin existed as a lake for a period of up to six thousand years, during which time the boulder berms formed along the old shoreline.

These berms also define the location of ten or so islands on the western side of the basin and a few small ones on the eastern side, which were submerged by the rising marine waters 5,800 years ago. Some of the islands have been previously named, such as Jonquière and Parfait Banks, named after the French fleet under Duke D'Anville that assembled and suffered disaster in the Basin in 1746. Additional names for some of the others—such as Sherwood Bank and Princes Lodge Bank—have been proposed through the Geological Survey of Canada.

At the sill area between Bedford Bay and Bedford Basin proper lies another critical site in the sea level story. On the nautical charts, it is presently known as Wellesley Rock. Here the seabed was exposed as land in a series of prominent bedrock ridges for the same period of time as the islands of the basin. Part of an early Sackville River cascaded in a waterfall over these ridges, connecting Bedford Bay to the basin. This waterfall and the surrounding bedrock ridges, together with the series of islands, represent former landscape elements that hold great archaeological potential. Given that this landscape coincided with the earliest era of human settlement and land use in the region (the Palaeo Period), investigation could yield important First Nations discoveries, including hieroglyphs and shell middens. The bedrock of the ridges is Goldenville quartzite, and its structure is oriented so that large surfaces would have previously been polished by the glaciers that moved from northwest to southeast through the region. It is not difficult to imagine the landscape of the time as a highly favourable site for fishing and habitation, as well as an ancient short cut across the basin. With plans to fill in some of this part of the basin for waterfront development projects, there is an urgent necessity for surveys of this archaeologically significant landscape to be conducted before such construction projects begin.

Two Shipwrecks off Point Pleasant Park

During the Halifax Harbour seabed mapping project, two unknown shipwrecks were discovered in the narrow entrance to the inner harbour, in an area between Ives Knoll (to the north of McNabs Island) and Pleasant Shoal (south of Point Pleasant Park). This

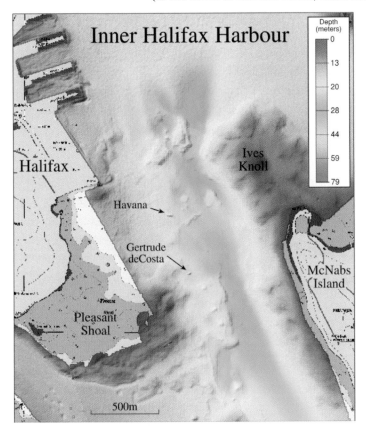

A colour-coded multibeam bathymetric map of the seabed of the inner part of Halifax Harbour, between the north of McNabs Island and Point Pleasant Park. Here the seabed is more complex than in areas to the north, and consists of current-scoured zones, bedrock, and erosional features. The shipwrecks of the Havana and Gertrude de Costa are clearly depicted. Water depths range up to thirty-eight metres.

is a dangerous navigational channel, as ships entering and leaving the harbour must pass in close proximity. The identification of the two shipwrecks took place over a five-year period and illustrates some of the problems in finding shipwrecks and making positive identifications.

The first vessel discovered with sidescan sonar lies to the southwest of Ives Knoll. From a study of the archives, it was initially believed to be the *Alexander R.*, a coal-ladened schooner that sank after collision with the steamer *Afranmore* in the harbour in 1906. Structures on the deck, such as open holds and compartments, are clearly defined on the sonar data. A dive to the wreck with an ROV quickly located the wooden ship lying partially on its side. The binnacle (where the ship's compass was housed) was encrusted with pink lithothamnia, a common coralline concretionary growth. The mast was found lying on the seabed with the goose neck attached where the boom was once connected.

Though researchers had believed the ship to be the *Alexander R.*, information from the Maritime Museum of the Atlantic soon called the identity of the wreck into question. The museum's records clearly reported that the *Alexander R.* had been refloated and its cargo of coal sold; the schooner then went on to spend many more years in service. After this setback, further archival research provided the true identity of the ship lying at the bottom of the harbour: the *Havana*. The *Havana* was a fifty-nine-metre salvage schooner owned by Captain J. A. Farquhar and was in the process of retrieving the *Alexander R.* when it was struck amidships by the steamer *Strathcona* on April 26, 1906. This scenario fit the damage seen on the sonar data. The *Havana* remained for a few minutes skewered by the *Strathcona*, long enough for the crew of the *Havana* to scramble to safety. Captain Farquhar was paid by Lloyd's insurance company for the sinking but forever lamented the loss of his most prized possession: a presentation sextant given to him by the British Admiralty for salvaging the guns of HMS *Niobe* in 1874. The sextant had traveled with him for many years around the world. He was quoted as saying: "If I did not have a year on my head for almost every foot below the surface in which my most prized possession lies, I would go down for it." Though a group of divers found an unadorned sextant in the area in 1991, it is believed that the presentation sextant remains on the wreck of the *Havana*, and that the recovered sextant belonged to another vessel.

Following the discovery of the *Havana*, Halifax diver Terry Dwyer conducted a series of official dives on the wreck for the Maritime Museum of the Atlantic. He found the wreck intact, with artifacts such as plates, cups, and bottles scattered about. A bell without markings was found at the stern and is now part of the collection of the Maritime Museum.

To this date, the *Havana* remains sitting in the busiest section of Halifax Harbour, continually passed over by ships entering and leaving the harbour. Situated just off of McNabs Island, the wreck is quite near the location originally proposed for an outfall from a sewage treatment plant on Ives Knoll. With that proposal since rejected, the shipwreck is protected from further damage. But what remains of Captain Farquhar's special presentation sextant? As it has yet to be found, it is possible that the remains of the *Havana* might reward further investigation.

Sidescan sonar records of the shipwrecks of the Havana (l) and Gertrude de Costa. Holds, hatches, and masts clearly appear on the decks.

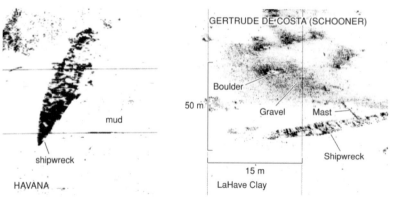

The second shipwreck in this area eluded detection for a very long time. In fact, despite two years of surveying the harbour, the wreck was overlooked due to traffic problems, navigational breakdowns, and equipment malfunctions. A small data gap resulted; and, as is often the case, the wreck was in the missing sector. It was only during a test cruise of the CCGS *Frederick G. Creed* in 1990 that this new shipwreck was discovered with sidescan sonar, east of Pleasant Shoal and south of the *Havana*. It appeared as a schooner-shaped vessel, approximately thirty metres in length, lying on a silty bottom.

A possible identity for the shipwreck presented itself when diver Terry Dwyer found headlines from the *Halifax Herald* newspaper, dated April 18, 1950, stating that a schooner had sunk in Halifax Harbour, with eleven men missing and presumed dead. The ship was the *Gertrude de Costa*, a fishing vessel returning from the Grand Banks early in the morning of April 18. Upon entering the narrow channel between Ives Knoll and Pleasant Shoal, the *Gertrude de Costa* collided with the *Island Connector*, a large steel freighter about to leave the harbour from Imperial Oil in Dartmouth. Most of the men

Porthole and corroded frame from the Havana. A diver took this photograph, which shows a large number of sea anemones on the wooded hull of the shipwreck.

were asleep below decks, and the schooner went down like a rock. Seven of the men scrambled to their feet, and though some got caught in the rigging, several of these managed to free themselves and rise to the surface of the frigid harbour waters. They were soon picked up by the crew of the *Island Connector*, who were later commended for their heroic rescue efforts. The military at once began a salvage operation to find the vessel and dragged the harbour bottom for days attempting to find the lost ship. It was never found.

Working on the hypothesis that the vessel discovered was the wreck of the *Gertrude de Costa*, sidescan sonar images collected from the area were consulted. The images documented at least four clear passes over the wreck. It was evident from the sonar records that the length and width of the wreck approximated the dimensions of the *Gertrude de Costa*. Furthermore, the large gash amidships indicated that the sunken ship had been in a collision.

With a permit from the Nova Scotia Museum, Terry Dwyer dove to the wreck in 1992. The images revealed clearer details of the sunken schooner than had been expected: the vessel appeared to be lying on its port side, in approximately thirty metres of water. A wooden schooner over thirty metres in length, both of its two masts had fallen to the seabed beside the wreck. Several batteries, a fire extinguisher, and an engine with a panel of gauges strongly suggested that the vessel was relatively modern; indeed, it had to be the *Gertrude de Costa*. There is a story that one of the survivors from the *Gertrude de Costa* left behind on the vessel the medals he had recently received for service in World War Two. These medals may still be there, along with the uncovered remains of the vessel crew.

The story of the discovery of the *Havana* and the *Gertrude de Costa*, so close to the shoreline of Halifax Harbour, illustrates how difficult it can be to locate—let alone identify—shipwrecks in even a well-protected and busy harbour. Given the likelihood that over a hundred shipwrecks lie on the bottom of the Halifax Harbour and at its mouth, there is a great potential for other important discoveries to be made. Some of these wrecks represent war graves; some contain ordnance, hydrocarbons, and other cargoes; and some may be early exploration vessels. They all represent seabed hazards to a wide range of activities. It is important for marine archaeologists to help locate, describe, and identify them—fortunately, the combination of ever-evolving technology and persistence will provide valuable keys to unravelling the history of our oceans.

Authors

David Christianson is curator of archaeology at the Nova Scotia Museum. Educated at Saint Mary's University and McMaster University, he has conducted research on archaeological topics pertaining to First Nations, fur trading, and Acadians. His present efforts are directed at the protection and public presentation of archaeological sites in Nova Scotia.

Greg Cochkanoff, who holds a BBA in accounting from Acadia University, is the president of Atlantic Catch Data Limited. As a sport diver and avocational archaeologist, he has authored fourteen papers based on investigations into Nova Scotia's shipwrecks and underwater heritage sites. His work has been featured in television shows, books, and exhibits in several museums, including the Maritime Museum of the Atlantic.

Katie Cottreau-Robins is a graduate of Saint Mary's University and Dalhousie University (DALTECH) who has worked in archaeology since 1983. She is a part-time instructor in historical archaeology at Saint Mary's and is particularly interested in the history of black Loyalists as evidenced in archeological, documentary, and architectural records.

Stephen A. Davis is professor of anthropology at Saint Mary's University and president of Davis Archaeological Consultants Limited. He has been practising historic and pre-(European) contact archaeology in Nova Scotia for more than thirty years. He is author of numerous books, articles, and reports on archaeology in the province.

Danny Dyke is archaeology and Geographic Information Systems technician at the Nova Scotia Museum of Natural History. He is an honours anthropology graduate of Saint Mary's University and proprietor of Arcadia Research and Archaeological Mapping. He has provided map overlay services for numerous archaeology projects and developed an archaeological site prediction model for the Nova Scotia Museum and the Nova Scotia Department of Natural Resources.

Dawn T. Erickson is president of Erickson's Research Limited, a property title-search company. An anthropology graduate of Saint Mary's University, she has worked on archaeological sites in Canada, Spain, and The United States.

Paul A. Erickson is professor of anthropology at Saint Mary's University. He is author of numerous articles and books about Halifax heritage. He is a past president of the Nova Scotia Archaeology Society and a past chairperson of the Halifax Regional Municipality Heritage Advisory Committee.

Gordon Fader is a marine geologist with the Geological Survey of Canada (Atlantic) at the Bedford Institute of Oceanography. He has conducted research on the geology of the offshore of southeastern Canada for more than thirty-five years, focusing on the glacial history of the offshore, the interpretation of seabed materials and processes, and the application of marine geology to a wide variety of projects. In his career, he has authored more than 280 scientific publications.

Earl Luffman was an archaeologist at Parks Canada for twenty-three years, before retiring in 2004. He has conducted archaeological investigations at both Citadel Hill and Georges Island.

April D. MacIntyre is an anthropology graduate student at Memorial University of Newfoundland. An honours anthropology graduate of Saint Mary's University, she has been working in contract archaeology since 1998 and has been involved in several archaeology projects in Halifax, including those at the Halifax Regional Municipality parkade and the Shubenacadie Canal.

Liam D. Murphy is assistant professor of anthropology at California State University, Sacramento. A native of Halifax, he is an honours anthropology graduate of Saint Mary's University and holds a PhD from Yale University. He is author of *Digging Up Halifax: The Problems and Promise of Archaeology in Metropolitan Nova Scotia.*

Laird Niven is owner of In Situ–Cultural Heritage Research Group. He is a contract archaeologist specializing in eighteenth- and nineteenth-century material culture and mortuary archaeology. He has been working in Nova Scotian archaeology for the past twenty years.

Michele Raymond grew up in Halifax and is convinced that the city is a national treasure. She is an editor and researcher with particular interests in the Northwest Arm and early Maritime music. She studied linguistics at Yale University and law at Dalhousie University and in 2003 was elected Member of the Legislative Assembly of Nova Scotia.

Fred Schwarz is partner of Black Spruce Heritage Services. He has conducted archaeological projects in Alberta, Labrador, Newfoundland, Nova Scotia, and Ecuador. His recent work has involved archaeological assessment and monitoring of Hurricane Juan remediation work in Point Pleasant Park, the Halifax Public Gardens, and Hemlock Ravine, and on McNabs Island.

Lynne Schwarz is partner of Black Spruce Heritage Services. She has conducted archaeological projects in Alberta, Labrador, Newfoundland, and Nova Scotia. Her recent work has involved archaeological assessment and monitoring of Hurricane Juan remediation work in Point Pleasant Park, the Halifax Public Gardens, and Hemlock Ravine, and on McNabs Island.

W. Bruce Stewart is president and senior consultant with Cultural Resource Management (CRM) Group Limited, located in Halifax. He has investigated a number of urban archaeological sites across Ontario as well as within the Halifax Regional Municipality. He is a founder and past executive director of the Cataraqui Archaeological Research Foundation in Kingston, Ontario, and a past president of the Nova Scotia Archaeology Society.

Paul Williams is currently completing his doctoral degree in geography at Queen's University. He has been a professional archaeologist for over twenty years and holds degrees in archaeology from Wilfrid Laurier University and Cardiff University. He has taught at Queen's University and Saint Mary's University. He is a past president of the Nova Scotia Archaeology Society.

David Williamson is the social studies department head at Halifax West High School. He developed and has taught a provincially approved high school course in archaeology. He is past president of the Nova Scotia Archaeology Society and coauthor of *Discovering Archaeology: An Activity Book for Young Nova Scotians.*

References

Introduction, Paul A. Erickson

Boutilier, Brenda, Paul Erickson, Denise Hansen, and David Williamson. *Discovering Archaeology: An Activity Book for Young Nova Scotians.* Halifax: Nova Scotia Archaeology Society, 1993.

Cantwell, Ann-Marie and Diana diZerega Wall. *Unearthing Gotham: The Archaeology of New York City.* New Haven, Connecticut: Yale University Press, 2002.

Cemeteries Protection Act, Statutes of Nova Scotia 1998, c. 9.

"Doing Archaeology in Minnesota: Urban Archaeology." http://www.fromsitetostory.org/sources/archinmn/archinmnurban.asp (18 August 2004).

Erickson, Paul A. "The New Underground: Urban Archaeology in Halifax." *New Maritimes* 6(8), 1988, pp. 15–16.

Mayne, Alan, and Tim Murray, editors. *The Archaeology of Urban Landscapes: Explorations in Slumland.* Cambridge, England: Cambridge University Press, 2002.

"Nova Scotia Archaeology Society." http://nsas.ednet.ns.ca/ (18 August 2004).

"Nova Scotia Museum Archaeology." http://museum.gov.ns.ca/arch/index.htm (18 August 2004).

Ottaway, Patrick. *Archaeology in British Towns.* London: Routledge, 1992.

Potter, Parker B. *Public Archaeology in Annapolis: A Critical Approach to History in Maryland's Ancient City.* Washington, DC: Smithsonian Institution Press, 1994.

Special Places Protection Act, Statutes of Nova Scotia 1989, c. 438.

Treasure Trove Act, Statutes of Nova Scotia 1989, c. 477.

"Urban Archaeology in Turkey." http://www.metu.edu.tr/home/wwwmuze/urban4.html (18 August 2004).

First Nations Archaeology in Halifax, David Christianson

Davis, Stephen A. "The Skora Site (BdCw-1)" in "Preliminary Research Permit Report No. A1987NS05." Halifax, Nova Scotia: Museum of Natural History, 1987.

"Heritage Resources Survey of McNab's Island " in "Heritage Research Permit Report No. A1991NS08." Halifax: Museum of Natural History, 1991.

Martin, John P. *The Story of Dartmouth.* Dartmouth, Nova Scotia: Privately Printed by the Author, 1957.

Molyneaux, Brian Leigh. "The Bedford Barrens Petroglyph Survey Project" in "Heritage Research Permit Report No. A1990NS18." Halifax, Nova Scotia: Museum of Natural History, 1990.

Piers, Harry. *Aboriginal Remains of Nova Scotia Illustrated by the Provincial Museum Collection.* Nova Scotia Institute of Science 7, 1879.

Sheldon, Helen. "A Shell Midden in Halifax Harbour" in "Archaeology in Nova Scotia 1992, 1993 and 1994" Curatorial Report No. 95. Halifax: Nova Scotia Museum, n.d.

Whitehead, Ruth Holmes. *The Harry Piers Ethnology Papers*, transcribed, edited and annotated by Ruth Holmes Whitehead. Halifax: Manuscript on file, Nova Scotia Museum of Natural History, 2003.

Plumbing the Past: Water and Sewage at Fort Charlotte and Fort George, Earl Luffman

Greenough, John Joseph. "The Halifax Citadel: 1825–60." Parks Canada, MRS No. 154, 1974.

Luffman, Earl J. *Archaeological Excavations at Fort Charlotte (Georges Island) 1991–1992*. Halifax, Nova Scotia: Parks Canada, 1993.

———. *Archaeological Inventory of Georges Island 1988*, revised edition. Halifax, Nova Scotia: Parks Canada, 2003.

MacLean, Terrance D. *George's Island 1749–1906*. Halifax, Nova Scotia: Parks Canada, n.d.

Marshall, Dianne. *Georges Island: The Keeper of Halifax Harbour*. Halifax, Nova Scotia: Nimbus Publishing Limited, 2003.

McDonald, Ronald H. *A Narrative and Structural History of the Redan*. Halifax, Nova Scotia: Parks Canada, 1982.

NovaScotian, 12 February 1851, p.41.

Parmenter, Caroline Phillips. "Salvage Archaeology at Halifax Citadel, Nova Scotia, September to November, 1976." Department of Indian and Northern Affairs, Parks Canada, MRS No. 231, 1975–1976.

Young, Richard J. "The West Front: Halifax Citadel." Department of Indian and Northern Affairs, Parks Canada, MRS No. 206, 1977.

The Central Trust Affair and Lessons Learned, April D. MacIntyre and Stephen A. Davis

Davis, Stephen A., Catherine Cottreau, and Laird Niven. *Artifacts from Eighteenth-Century Halifax*. Halifax: Saint Mary's University, 1987.

"Goad's Insurance Plan for Halifax City, 1895." Nova Scotia Archives and Records Management, Map Collection V6/240.

"Hopkins Land Use Atlas of Halifax, 1878." Nova Scotia Archives and Records Management, Map Collection V6/240.

Special Places Protection Act, Statutes of Nova Scotia 1989, c. 438.

Vaudreuil, Philippe de Rigaud de. "A Plan of Halifax with a scheme of attacking it from Canaday…." Public Records Office, London. S.P.42/38, p.224.

Wentworth, Henry, Lieutenant Royal Engineers. "General Plan of the Town of Halifax, Nova Scotia. Public Records Office, London. WO55/2594 L BP704.

Samuel Sellon's Grandmother's House, Dawn T. Erickson

Erickson, Paul A. *Halifax's North End: An Anthropologist Looks at the City.* Hantsport, Nova Scotia: Lancelot Press, 1986.

Erickson, Paul A., Dawn Mitchell, Laird Niven, Katie Cottreau, and Nicola Hubbard. "Sellon Site (BdCv: 7)" in "Archaeology in Nova Scotia 1985 and 1986 (1987)." Nova Scotia Museum Curatorial Report 63, pp.9–75.

"Goad's Insurance Plan for Halifax City, 1895." Nova Scotia Archives and Records Management, Map Collection V6/240.

Hubbard, Nicola. "Archaeology in the City of Halifax." Manuscript on file at the Department of Development, City of Halifax, 1985.

Mitchell, Dawn. "Digging the North End" in *Halifax's North End: An Anthropologist Looks at the City*, Paul Erickson. Hantsport, Nova Scotia: Lancelot Press, 1986, pp.123–128.

Murphy, Liam. "Digging Up Halifax: The Problems and Promise of Archaeology in Metropolitan Nova Scotia" in *Saint Mary's University Occasional Papers in Anthropology* 17. Halifax: Saint Mary's University, 1994.

Noel Hume, Ivor. *A Guide to Artifacts of Colonial America.* New York: Alfred A. Knopf, 1982.

"Sellon Family Genealogy." Manuscript in possession of Dawn Erickson, 1986.

Avoiding the Bulldozer: Archival Resources for Archaeology Downtown, Liam D. Murphy

Chronicle-Herald, 6 May 1976, p. 14.

Fingard, Judith. *The Dark Side of Life in Victorian Halifax.* Porters Lake, Nova Scotia: Pottersfield Press, 1989.

"Land Registration and Information Services of Nova Scotia." Microfiche No. 5P11-04NW. Property Allotment Map of Halifax, 1991.

Murphy, Liam. "Digging Up Halifax: The Problems and Promise of Archaeology in Metropolitan Nova Scotia" in *Saint Mary's University Occasional Papers in Anthropology* 17. Halifax: Saint Mary's University, 1994.

Nova Scotia Archives and Records Management. Microfilm Collection: Places, V6/240. Halifax Allotment Book, 1749.

———. Map Collection, V6/240, 1755.

———. MG 100, Vol. 52, No. 40, 1755.

———. MG 100, Vol. 51, No. 48, 1755.

———. MG 10, Vol. 23, No. 55, 1787.

———. "Hopkins Land Use Atlas of Halifax, 1878."

———. Map Collection, V6/240, 1879.

———. Map Collection, V6/240, 1890.

————. Map Collection, V6/240, 1945.

————. Fire Insurance Plans, 1965.

Nova Scotia Registry of Deeds. Lease: 28/296, 1788.

Nova Scotia Registry of Deeds. Deed: 42/333, 1816.

Nova Scotia Registry of Deeds. Will: 381/58, 1901.

Raddall, Thomas H. *Halifax: Warden of the North*, revised edition. Toronto: McClelland and Stewart, 1971.

What Maps Can Show Us, Danny Dyke

DesBarres, Joseph Frederick Wallet. "The Harbour of Halifax." Library and Archives of Canada, NMC18457, 1778.

Dyke, Danny. "Archaeology and GIS in Halifax: A Demonstration of the Utility of GIS as a Research Tool." Honours Thesis, Saint Mary's University, 2001.

Fingard, Judith. "Robie Street Halifax" in *Halifax Street Names: An Illustrated Guide,"* ed. Shelagh MacKenzie with Scott Robson. Halifax: Formac Publishing, 2002, pp.183–185.

Hopkins, E., Sgt. "Halifax Sheet IV.10." Library and Archives of Canada, NMC8457, 1886.

Moorsom, William, Capt. "52nd Reg. Harbour of Halifax Nova Scotia." National Archives of London, ref. MR 1/143(3), 1827.

Straton, James, Capt. Royal Engineers. "Plan of Harbour of Halifax." National Archives of London, ref. MR 1/384(1), 1796.

Tales from the Crypt: Excavations Beneath the Little Dutch Church, Paul Williams

Anonymous. *A Brief History of the Little Dutch Church (St. George's),* 1899.

Ariés, Philippe. *The Hour of Our Death.* Harmondsworth, England: Penguin Books, 1987.

Erickson, Paul A. "All that Remains: The Saga of Human Burials Beneath the Little Dutch Church in Halifax." Manuscript in possession of Paul Williams, 1999.

Fergusson, C. B. *A Documentary Study of the Establishment of the Negroes in Nova Scotia Between the War of 1812 and the Winning of Responsible Government.* Publication No. 8. Halifax: Public Archives of Nova Scotia, 1948.

Lundrigan, Nicole. "Analysis of Skeletal Material Recovered Beneath the Little Dutch Church." Manuscript in possession of Paul Williams, 1996.

Niven, Laird. *Little Dutch Church Project, 1998.* Manuscript submitted to the Nova Scotia Museum, 1998.

Niven, Laird, and Paul B. Williams. *Little Dutch Church Project, 1996.* Manuscript submitted to the Nova Scotia Museum, 1997.

Nova Scotia Archives and Records Management. MG1, Vol. 238, No. 3B. C.E. Thomas, Rev. Bernard Michael Houseal, M.A. 1727-1799, pp. 3,7.

————. Reel ll551X, Saint Paul's Anglican Church Records, n.d., p. 27.

Pacey, Elizabeth. *Miracle on Brunswick Street: The Story of St. George's Round Church and the Little Dutch Church.* Halifax: Nimbus Publishing, 2003.

Pross, Catherine. "Schwartz, Otto William (Otto Wilhelm)" in *Dictionary of Canadian Biography*, Vol. 4, pp. 703–704.

Location, Location, Location! Archaeological Mitigation on the Halifax Wastewater Treatment Property, W. Bruce Stewart

Cultural Resource Management Group Ltd. "Archaeological Screening Proposed STP Site Barrington/Cornwallis/Upper Water Streets, Halifax: Archaeological Screening Report." Report on file with the Nova Scotia Museum, 1999.

———— "Archaeological Assessment Halifax Sewage Treatment Plant Property, Halifax, Nova Scotia: Archaeological Impact Assessment—Final Report." Report on file with the Nova Scotia Museum, 2002.

———— "Archaeological Mitigation on the Halifax Wastewater Treatment Plant Property BdCv-35, Halifax, Nova Scotia, Archaeological Impact Assessment Final Report." Report on file with the Nova Scotia Museum, 2004.

A Walk in the Park: Point Pleasant Park after Hurricane Juan, Lynne Schwarz and Fred Schwarz

Blaskowitz, Charles. "Plan of the Peninsula upon which the Town of Halifax is situated." Nova Scotia Archives and Records Management Map Collection V6/240-1784.

Greenough, J. Outforts. "Section 3: Point Pleasant Park." Draft typescript on file at Parks Canada, 1977.

Kitz, Janet and Gary Castle. *Point Pleasant Park: An Illustrated History*. Halifax: Pleasant Point Publishing, 1999.

Mercer, Colonel A.C. "Watercolour Sketch." Nova Scotia Archives and Records Management, Photo Collection No. 6170b, 1842.

Piers, Harry. *The Evolution of the Halifax Fortress: 1749-1928*, revised edition. Halifax: Public Archives of Nova Scotia, 1947.

Stewart, Colin. Unpublished notes in possession of Lynne Schwarz and Fred Schwarz, n.d.

Deadmans Island: Preserving the Past for the Future, Michele Raymond

Deveau, J. Alphonse, editor. *Diary of a Frenchman: François Lambert Bourneuf's Adventures from France to Acadia, 1787-1871*. Halifax: Nimbus Publishing, 1990.

Haliburton, Thomas Chandler. *An Historical and Statistical Account of Nova Scotia*. Halifax: Joseph Howe, 1829.

Watts, Heather and Michelle Raymond. *The Northwest Arm: An Illustrated History*. Halifax: Formac Publishing, 2003.

Along the Shubenacadie Canal, Stephen A. Davis and April D. MacIntyre

Barnett, Donna. *River of Dreams: The Saga of the Shubenacadie Canal*. Halifax: Nimbus Publishing, 2002.

Davis, Stephen A., ed. "Shubenacadie Canal Redevelopment: Archaeological Survey, Zone 3." Manuscript on file at the Nova Scotia Museum of Natural History, 1985.

Haliburton, Thomas Chandler. *A Historical and Statistical Account of Nova Scotia, in Two Volumes: Illustrated by a Map of the Province and Several Engravings*. Halifax, Nova Scotia: Joseph Howe, 1829.

Moorsom, William. *Letters from Nova Scotia: comprising sketches of a young country*. London: Henry Colburn and Richard Bentley, 1830.

Passfield, Robert W. *The Shubenacadie Canal*. Ottawa: Historic Sites and Monuments Board of Canada and Parks Canada, 1979.

Russell, William A. "One Mile of Canal: An Historical Overview of Land Use at the Summit Section 2, the Shubenacadie Canal." In Stephen A. Davis, ed., "Shubenacadie Canal Redevelopment: Archaeological Survey, Zone 3." Manuscript on file at the Nova Scotia Museum of Natural History, 1985.

Special Places Protection Act, Revised Statutes of Nova Scotia 1989, c. 438.

Excavation of Seaview African United Baptist Church, Africville,
Katie Cottreau-Robins

Brooks, Bob. Photographs, Acc. 1989-468, Box 16, Files 146 and 147. Nova Scotia Archives and Records Management, n.d.

Clairmont, Donald. "Africville: An Historical Overview" in Africville Genealogy Society, ed., *The Spirit of Africville*, Halifax: Formac Publishing Company, 1992, pp.36–50.

Clairmont, Donald. *Africville: The Life and Death of a Canadian Black Community*. Toronto: Canadian Scholars Press, 1987.

Clairmont, Donald H. and Dennis W. Magill. "Africville Relocation Report." Halifax: Institute of Public Affairs, Dalhousie University, 1971.

Cottreau-Robins, Catherine. "Excavation of the Seaview African United Baptist Church, Africville" in "Archaeology in Nova Scotia 1992, 1993, and 1994." Curatorial Report No. 95. Halifax: Nova Scotia Museum, n.d., pp.56–70.

Davis, S., C. Lindsay, R. Ogilvie, and B. Preston, editors. "Archaeology in Nova Scotia 1987 and 1988." Curatorial Report No. 69. Halifax: Nova Scotia Department of Education, 1991.

Fladmark, Knut R. *A Guide to Basic Archaeological Field Procedures*. Publication No. 4. Burnaby, British Columbia: Department of Archaeology, Simon Fraser University, 1978.

Kimber, Stephen. "Taking Back the Neighborhood." *Canadian Geographical Magazine* 112 (4), 1992.

Remember Africville. Halifax: National Film Board of Canada, Atlantic Centre, 1989.

Sanders, Charles R., ed. *Africville: A Spirit that Lives On*. Halifax: Art Gallery of Mount Saint

Vincent University, Black Cultural Centre of Nova Scotia, Africville Genealogy Society, and National Film Board of Canada, Atlantic Centre, 1989.

"The Other Africville." *Cities*, October 1989, pp. 19–23.

The Rockingham Inn Project, David Williamson

"All the Queen's Men: Edward Duke of Kent 1767-1820." http://www.pbs.org/wgbh/masterpiece/mbrown/men/edward_bio.html (20 August 2004).

"Biographies: Governor Sir John Wentworth 1737-1820." http://www.blupete.com/Hist/BiosNS/1764-00/Wentworth.htm (20 August 2004).

Carter, Howard. *The Tomb of Tutankhamen*. London: Sphere Books, 1972.

Comiter, Alvin and Elizabeth Pacey. *Historic Halifax*. Willowdale, Ontario: Hounslow Press, 1988.

Fingard, Judith, Janet Guildford, and Donald Sutherland. *Halifax: The First 250 Years*. Halifax: Formac Publishing Company, 1999.

"Halifax City." http://www3.ns.sympatico.ca/bryanfkeddy/ (20 August 2004).

"Hemlock Ravine Management Plan July 7, 2000." http://www.cpawsns.org/HRPMP/hrpmptoc.htm (20 August 2004).

"Hilroy Fellowship Program Innovations '95." Ottawa, Ontario: Canadian Teachers Federation, 1995.

McCreath, Peter and John C. Leefe. *History of Early Nova Scotia*. Tantallon, Nova Scotia: Four East Publications, 1983.

Payzant, Joan. *Halifax: Cornerstone of Canada*. Windsor Publications Canada, 1985.

Raddall, Thomas. *Halifax: Warden of the North*. Toronto: McClelland & Stewart, 1971.

Williams, Paul. "Rockingham Inn Project Oct. 1994. Permit Number A1994NS24." Manuscript on file at the Nova Scotia Museum of Natural History, n.d.

———. "The Rockingham Inn Project 1995: Interim Report. Permit Number A1995NS26." Halifax: Nova Scotia Museum of Natural History, 1995.

A Day at the Beach: The Coote Cove Archaeology Project, Laird Niven

Longard, Evelyn Nickerson. "History of Coote Cove, Halifax County, Nova Scotia." Unpublished speech, 1966.

Longard, Evelyn Nickerson and Rev. B.R. Tupper. *Historical Sketch of St. James United Church, Sambro, Nova Scotia*. Sambro, Nova Scotia: Saint James United Church, n.d.

Noel Hume, Ivor. *A Guide to Artifacts of Colonial America*. New York: Alfred A. Knopf, 1982.

Powell, Stephen T. *Archaeological Survey of Sandy Bay Provincial Park, Cole Harbour Day Use Park and Crystal Crescent Beach Provincial Park–1990*. Halifax: Department of Lands and Forests, 1990.

Sussman, Lynne. *Mocha, Banded, Cat's Eye, and Other Factory-Made Slipware*. Boston: Council for Northeast Historical Archaeology, 1997.

Tuck, James. *Maritime Provinces Prehistory*. Ottawa: National Museum of Man, 1984.

Walker, Iain. *Ontario Archaeology* 16, 1971.

Steamship China from Halifax Harbour, Greg Cochkanoff

Appleton, Thomas E. *Ravenscraig: The Allan Royal Mail Line*. Toronto: McClelland and Stewart, 1974.

Bonsor, N.R.P. *North Atlantic Seaway*. Brookside Publications, 1980.

Brinnin, John M. *The Sway of the Grand Saloon*. New York: Delacorte Press, 1971.

Chaulk, Bob. *Time in a Bottle: Historic Halifax Harbour from the Bottom Up*. Lawrencetown Beach, Nova Scotia: Pottersfield Press, 2002.

Cochkanoff, Greg. *Royal Navy China of Halifax Harbour*. Privately published, 2004.

———. *Steamship China of Halifax Harbour*, Volumes I and II. Privately published, 2004.

Keir, David. *The Bowring Story*. London: The Bodley Head, 1962.

The Marine Archaeology of Halifax Harbour, Gordon Fader

Chronicle Herald, 18 July 1989, pp.1, 20.

Courtney, R. C. and G. B. J. Fader. "A New Understanding of the Ocean Floor Through Multibeam Mapping" in *Science Review 1992 and 1993*. Dartmouth, Nova Scotia: Bedford Institute of Oceanography, Department of Fisheries and Oceans, 1994, pp.9–14.

Fader, G. B. J. and D. E. Buckley. "Marine Geology and Geochemistry in the Environmental Management of Halifax Harbour" in *Environmental Geology of Urban Regions*. Special Publication of the Geological Association of Canada, GeoText 3, 1997, pp.249–267.

Fader, G. B. J. and R. O. Miller. "Discovery Of a New Shipwreck Heritage in Halifax Harbour and Adjacent Areas: Technology, Conflict and Implications." Abstract. Halifax: Society for the Preservation of Natural History, 10 July 2000.

Fader, G. B. J., R. O. Miller, and A. Craft. "Bedford Basin: Nova Scotia: An Interpretation of Seabed Materials, Features and Processes on Multibeam Bathymetry." Geological Survey of Canada Open File Report No. 3941, 2001.

Fader, G. B. J., R. O. Miller, and S. S. Pecore. "The Marine Geology of Halifax Harbour and Adjacent Areas," Volumes 1 and 2. Geological Survey of Canada Open File Report No. 2384, 1991.

Fader, G. B. J. and B. Petrie. "Halifax Harbour—How the Currents Affect Sediment Distributions" in Thea E. Smith, ed., *Science Review 1988 and 1989*. Dartmouth, Nova Scotia: The Halifax Fisheries Research Laboratory and the St. Andrews Biological Station, Scotia-Fundy Region of the Department of Fisheries and Oceans, Bedford Institute of Oceanography, 1991, pp. 31–35.

Miller, R. O. and G. B. J. Fader. *The Bottom of Halifax Harbour*. Geological Survey of Canada Open File Report No. 3154, 1995.

Image Credits

Barnett, Donna, 90, 100
Canadian Forces Base Summerside, 12
Chronicle-Herald, 137
Cochkanoff, Greg, 124, 125a, 125b, 126, 127, 128, 130, 131, 132a, 132b, 133, 134
Cottreau-Robins, Katie, 18, 20, 21, 102, 103a, 103b, 104, 105a, 105b, 105c
CRM Group Limited, 63, 68, 69a, 69b, 69c, 70a, 70b, 70c, 71a, 71b, 72
Davis, Stephen A., 22a, 22b, 23, 90, 95, 96, 98
Dwyer, Terry, 145
Erickson, Dawn and Paul Erickson, 28, 29a, 29b, 31, 32
Fader, Gordon, 139b, 142
Fowler, Jonathan, 114b
Geological Survey of Canada and Canadian Hydrographic Service, 135 (with Gordon Fader), 138,
    141, 143, 144
Haliburton, Thomas Chandler, 92a
Halifax Citadel Collection, 11b
Hueber, Brent, 58a
Library and Archives of Canada, 11a, 25, 50, 51 (with Danny Dyke), 52 (with Danny Dyke), 129
Luffman, Earl, 14a
MacIntyre, April D., 99
MacMaster, Michael, 56
Maritime Command Museum, 19, 25
Murphy, Liam D., 34
The National Archives, London, 47, 48, 49 (with Nova Scotia Museum of Natural History)
Niven, Laird, 57, 59a, 59b, 115, 116, 119, 120, 121, 122
Nova Scotia Archives and Records Management, 10, 27a, 27b, 33, 36, 37a, 37b, 39, 42, 55a, 55b,
    55c, 67, 77, 81, 82, 85, 86, 88, 92b, 93, 94, 101, 108, 109, 139a
Nova Scotia Department of Natural Resources, 74
Nova Scotia Museum, 1, 3, 4a, 4b, 6
Parks Canada, 8, 14b, 14c, 16
Parks Canada Citadel, 78
Schwarz, Fred, 73, 76, 79, 80
Stevens, Elizabeth, 106
University of Virginia, 11c
Williams, Paul, 54, 58b
Williamson, David, 110b, 112a, 112b, 113a, 113b, 113c, 114a